Creating Vacation
Scrapbook Pages

MEMORY
MAKERS
BOOKS

D1377212

EXECUTIVE EDITOR Kerry Arquette   FOUNDER Michele Gerbrandt

EDITOR Emily Curry Hitchingham
ART DIRECTOR Andrea Zocchi
DESIGNER Nick Nyffeler
ART ACQUISITIONS EDITOR Janetta Abucejo Wieneke
CRAFT EDITOR Jodi Amidei
PHOTOGRAPHER Ken Trujillo
CONTRIBUTING PHOTOGRAPHERS Brenda Martinez, Christina Dooley, Kelli Noto, Terry Ownby, Jennifer Reeves
ART CAPTION WRITER Nicole Cummings
EDITORIAL SUPPORT Karen Cain, MaryJo Regier, Lydia Rueger, Dena Twinem

Memory Makers® Creating Vacation Scrapbook Pages

Published by Memory Makers Books, an imprint of F&W Publications, Inc.
12365 Huron Street, Suite 500, Denver, CO 80234
Phone 1-800-254-9124
First edition. Printed in the United States.
08 07 06 05 04 5 4 3 2 1

Library of Congress Cataloging-in-Publication Data

Creating vacation scrapbook pages.
     p. cm.
  ISBN 1-892127-29-6
   1. Photographs--Conservation and restoration. 2. Photograph albums. 3. Scrapbooks. 4.
  Travel photography. 5. Vacations I. Memory Makers Books.

  TR465.C74 2004
  745.593--dc22

                                            2004040243

Distributed to trade and art markets by
F & W Publications, Inc.
4700 East Galbraith Road, Cincinnati, OH 45236
Phone 1-800-289-0963

ISBN 1-892127-29-6
Memory Makers Books is the home of *Memory Makers*, the scrapbook magazine dedicated to educating and inspiring scrapbookers. To subscribe, or for more information, call 1-800-366-6465.
Visit us on the Internet at www.memorymakersmagazine.com

This book belongs to

_____

We dedicate this book to all of our Memory Makers contributors
who graciously shared their stunning travel scrapbook pages with us,
and to adventure seekers everywhere.

Table of Contents

Shoreside Escapes
14-37

Wet and wild page ideas devoted to aquatic-inspired vacations. Includes layouts featuring sun-soaked sandy beaches, wave-lapped lakesides, luxury cruise liners, rugged whitewater rafting, surf-skipping water crafts, smooth summertime sails, beneath-the-blue snorkeling and more.

Outdoor Adventures
38-59

Awe-inspiring page ideas dedicated to the wide open wild frontier. Includes layouts featuring are-we-almost-there road trips, quiet camping and cabin retreats, serene streamside fishing, summit-minded mountain hikes, pristine powdered ski slopes, unspoiled off-trail terrain and more.

Eye-Opening
Excursions 60–81

Innovative page ideas inspired by free-falling fun and educational enrichment. Includes layouts featuring favorite family theme parks, exotic aquariums and animal sanctuaries, mind-expanding museums and memorials, and step-back-in-time historical sights.

America
the Beautiful 82–103

Outstanding page ideas that pay homage to the land of the free and the home of the brave. Includes layouts that celebrate America's incredible cities, unforgettable sights and star-spangled spirit from sea to shining sea.

International Intrigue
104–125

Extraordinary page ideas that exhibit the wondrous destinations that await around the world. Includes layouts that boast the breathtaking beauty, inspiring culture and rich history that herald from places beyond our home borders.

BON VOYAGE

Adventure

RELAX

BON VOYAGE

Family Reunion 2003

No dishes, no chores ..."Mom, what will you do with yourself?", my kids asked. We had 30 family members all together for a 7-day cruise in the Caribbean. We had the chance to spend more time with each other than we had in 20 years. Here are the kids on "formal night"...they know it's photo op time!!!

Anna

Sasha

Daniel

Introduction

Travel has the potential for some of the fondest memories. If only for a little while, we are removed from our day-to-day responsibilities and obligations and given the opportunity to enjoy exciting new places and interesting people. In traveling, we enact our desires to learn, explore, relax and appreciate simply being in the moment. The places we visit supply us with splendid views of the world beyond our backdoors and memories that become lasting and meaningful souvenirs.

For that very reason, it is important that we chronicle our travel experiences, whether they be returns down often-traveled roads leading to our childhood homes or excursions to places we've never seen before. Capturing the spirit of our adventures in our scrapbooks allows us to revisit beloved places again and again years after we've returned home.

While enjoying the wonderful ideas, techniques and beautiful layouts inside *Creating Vacation Scrapbook Pages*, you'll come to realize that this compilation is more than just an idea gallery dedicated to travel. It is evidence of the desire of scrapbookers to not only journey beyond their borders, but also to boldly explore new approaches to the creation of their scrapbook pages. This book is intended to open your eyes to new scrapbooking horizons with plenty of helpful prompts, from packing for your trip with your vacation layouts in mind, to travel journaling ideas and helpful checklists to keep you on target and assist you in identifying those don't-miss photo and memorabilia opportunities. The outstanding scrapbook pages featured will undoubtedly prove to be sources of inspiration for both your own vacation layouts, and perhaps even your next trip.

So get ready to cross several continents as seen through the eyes of scrapbookers around the globe. We'll visit pristine beaches, majestic mountaintops, unspoiled open spaces, sophisticated cities, and intriguing parks, museums and other points of interest. Have fun and enjoy the journey!

Michele

Michele Gerbrandt
Founding Editor
Memory Makers magazine

Photo and Memorabilia Checklists

You can be sure to bring more back from your vacation than just your memories with the help of these photo and memorabilia checklists. Venturing out on your vacation with a bit of organization and objective in mind will make later scrapbooking of your mementos a more manageable task.

Photography Checklist

Getting there: airports, train trips, car rides, ferries

Establishing shots of all destinations

Accommodations and favorite staff

Restaurants visited

Out on the town

Nightlife

Skylines day and night

Underwater fun

Outdoor explorations

Architecture

Points of interest

Local wildlife

Historical landmarks

Local people, culture and customs

Road signs, city limit signs, historical markers

Homebound travels

Memorabilia Checklist

Tickets: plane, train, theme parks, theatre, museums, etc.

Brochures

Programs

Maps

Foreign currency

Foreign postage stamps

Receipts from purchases and expenses

Paper napkins, place mats, coasters, matchbooks

Local flora

Sand

Seashells

Postcards

When putting memorabilia such as brochures, tickets, postcards and the like into your scrapbook, it should be assumed the items are acidic. To be certain, you may easily test acidity with a pH pen. If the levels of acidity exceed 7.5-8.5 pH, photocopy the item onto acid-free paper or mist it with an acid-neutralizing archival spray available from scrapbook supply stores. Newspaper clippings contain high amounts of lignin and acid and should be acid-neutralized and housed away from other memorabilia and photos. For three-dimensional memorabilia such as seashells or foreign currency, consider encapsulating the items in purchased or homemade memorabilia pockets, envelopes, shaker boxes, or plastic three-dimensional memorabilia keepers. Housing your memorabilia in these items will protect both your tokens of travel and surrounding photos.

Basic Tools and Supplies

The wealth of tools, supplies and products available today are nearly as diverse and abundant as your choice of travel destinations. Mapping out your scrapbook pages before beginning to shop for supplies will help you navigate your way through both the scrapbooking store and page-creating process.

Albums and scrapbook pages

Page protectors

Colored, printed and textured papers

Pigment pens and markers

Permanent and removable adhesives

Ruler

Scissors

Craft knife

Unique Design Additions

Die cuts

Stamps

Stickers

Punches

Templates

Memorabilia keepers

Photo corners

Paper trimmers/cutters

Specialty papers

Stencils

Clay

Fibers

Eyelets

Brads

Beads

Metals

For preservation purposes, we highly recommend the use of acid- and lignin-free albums and paper products, photo-safe adhesives, PVC-free plastics and pigment inks.

Taking Exceptional Travel Photographs

After the vacation is over, one final destination point remains on any travel itinerary: the local photo developer. We anticipate our photo souvenirs of our vacations almost as eagerly as we did our departure dates. The most lasting and convincing testimony of our travels, vacation photos that suspend our adventures forever in time are treasures for vacation scrapbooks. Keep in mind the following pointers and you'll hardly find the need to narrate your vacation photos—they will speak volumes for themselves.

FILL THE FRAME WITH YOUR SUBJECT
One of the oldest tricks in the book for taking wow-factor photos rather than merely decent shots is to fill the frame with your subject. Once you feel like you are close enough, move a few steps closer.

WHEN TO USE HORIZONTAL FORMATS
Use horizontal framing for wide scenes and long, squat subjects. This framing encourages the eye to sweep across the photo from side to side, emphasizing width and spaciousness.

COMPOSE YOUR SHOT USING THE RULE OF THIRDS
Resist the natural tendency to plant your subject squarely in the middle of the frame. Instead, divide the viewfinder into imaginary thirds horizontally and vertically like a tick-tack-toe board. Place your subject at any of the four intersections to create a dynamic shot.

WHEN TO USE VERTICAL FORMATS
Use vertical framing for tall subjects and for exaggerating distance. Formatting your photo this way leads the eye from top to bottom and bottom to top, reinforcing a sense of depth and distance.

INCLUDE PEOPLE TO ESTABLISH SCALE

Large-scale subjects such as mountains, the Mayan ruins, the giant sequoia trees and the Egyptian pyramids are even more impressive when you include people to reinforce the grandness of their size.

USE A TELEPHOTO LENS

Make them wonder how you got that incredible shot by using a telephoto lens to capture distant subjects without compromising spontaneity.

EXPERIMENT WITH DRAMATIC ANGLES

Move beyond the flat straight-on shot by physically moving to a unique vantage point. Snap your subject from an unexpected high, low or extreme lateral position to produce striking results.

WHEN TO USE PANORAMIC FORMATS

Utilize this dramatic framing to capture the vastness of scenes such as bridges, seascapes, landscapes and city skylines. Be sure to keep the horizon level and near the center of the frame to prevent the horizon line from appearing to "bend" from too high or low a placement. Don't forget to try panoramic shots in vertical formats as well.

Guide to Beginning Your Vacation Scrapbook

Whether you've got your sights set on a new travel destination or are returning to past adventures, creating vacation scrapbook pages is a trip for the imagination. Embarking on this endeavor with a little planning and organization will ensure that when it comes to creating exceptional travel layouts, getting there really is half the fun.

1. Don't Leave Home Without These Scrapbooking Supplies

Tickets? Check. Luggage? Check. In the midst of travel madness it is easy to forget any array of essentials. Be sure to have these basics on hand before hitting the road.

- Camera: Browse your owner's manual to refresh your memory as to your camera's special features and capabilities. Change the batteries and bring an extra pack, or if digital, a battery charger and additional memory card. Small, affordable, easy-to-pack tripods are a good idea to ensure no one from your travel party is missing from your photos. Consider also one-time use and underwater cameras.

- Film, and lots of it: Rule of thumb says at least a roll for every day that you will be traveling. Don't risk having to put sightseeing on hold to hunt down more film while on vacation where it will likely be more expensive. By keeping your camera and undeveloped film in plastic bags in your carry-on luggage and requesting hand inspections at airport checkpoints, you can help prevent any potential damage posed by x-ray scanning equipment.

- Journaling items: Carry a small bound journal and pens with you while traveling to record precious memories that will be included in future scrapbook pages. This journal may also be used to keep track of photos taken. A mini tape recorder can be used in addition to, or in place of, a written journal. Memory buttons are another great way to record the hustle and bustle of a downtown marketplace, the sounds of ethnic music, or a personal reflection on sights seen.

- Memorabilia storage: Plastic envelopes, manila folders, labels, permanent markers and resealable plastic bags are several inexpensive and easy-to-pack items to help protect, organize and transport your tokens of travel. Sorting and dating your memorabilia and film with these items will make later scrapbooking a more manageable process.

- Carrying bag: Comfortable shoulder bags, waist packs or backpacks that are not too bulky or heavy and have adequate storage pockets are must-haves for the traveling scrapbooker. Small locks can be purchased for added security.

2. Organize Photos and Memorabilia

Before you begin creating your layouts, organize your photos and group them chronologically. You may eventually choose to separate pictures and memorabilia by themes or events, but organizing in chronological fashion will make finding photos and remembering the progression of the trip easier. For optimum efficiency, create page kits for layouts that have been pre-planned and organized into page protectors. You may include a sketch and jotted notes detailing the design you have envisioned. Since page kits contain memorabilia and photos, store them upright and vertically, and house them inside a protective folder or binder. In organizing this way, you need only transfer the items from each pre-sorted plastic sleeve into actual layouts when ready.

3. Select an Album

Choose from three-ring binder, spiral-bound, post-bound or strap-hinge albums. The most popular and widely available sizes are 12 x 12" and 8½ x 11". Albums that are sturdy, soundly constructed and expandable are best for withstanding time and hundreds of viewings. Additionally, slipping your layouts into page protectors will ensure extra-long life for your pages. Always be sure to select archival-quality albums with acid- and lignin-free papers and PVC-free plastics.

4. Creating Vacation Layouts

Clean and uncomplicated, streamlined and simple, artsy and elaborate or a full-blown frame-worthy master-piece, your approach to scrapbook design is entirely up to you. While there are no hard and fast rules, here are a few tried and true tips for achieving aesthetically pleasing pages:

- Focal point: Feature an exceptional or unique focal photo by giving it a dominant position on the page, building secondary photos and page accents around it.

- Composition: Select colors, papers and embellishments that complement, not distract from, your photos. Remember to feature a title and leave room to journal.

- Photo cropping: Emphasize subject matter and eliminate flaws by cropping out busy or unnecessary backgrounds. Crop with caution to make certain you will not regret losing elements you have cut away.

- Matting and framing: Mounting your photos on mats or underneath frames created with papers, cutting tools and templates helps to showcase special shots and adds a crisp finishing touch.

- Embellishments: Explore the possibilities and have fun with the extensive array of design elements such as die cuts, stickers, punched shapes and more.

5. Journaling

Photographs will preserve the visual aspects of your travels, but little else. If done well, your journaling will ensure that your vacation memories remain rich and vivid indefinitely. Ponder these suggested approaches before putting pen to paper.

- Keep a chronological log of each day: Consistently detail what you did, where you went, what you saw, who you met, what you liked best, and what you would and wouldn't do next time guarantees no memory will be forgotten.

- Take down facts, history and trivia you find interesting: Make sure the miles you logged sightseeing and educating yourself are represented in your scrapbook pages.

- Tell a story: Recall the progression of events in a detailed and engaging narrative. Remember to include the mishaps and silly misadventures as well.

- Utilize quotes, poems and sayings: Add eloquence to your pages by calling on the works of others for creative inspiration.

- Employ thick description: Paint a picture with words as significant and engaging as your photographs. Pictures don't have to be the only sources of imagery.

- Incorporate the five senses: In recalling the sights, sounds, tastes, touches and smells of your travel experiences, you return to them in the pages of your travel album years after you've returned home.

- Be a journalist: Create newsworthy travel layouts by providing answers to the following questions at each destination point: who, what, when, where and why?

- Write home: Mail postcards to yourself from the road for a fun instant journaling technique.

- Review and reflect: Have everyone involved in the trip muse on what he or she thought of the vacation. This is especially meaningful if done in each person's original handwriting.

ANNEX STATION

VOLUSIA'S SEA TURTLES

volusia's sea turtles

FROM APRIL 1½ THROUGH OCT

from april 15 through oct

UNUSUAL MARINE VISITOR —

unusual marine visitor —

ANIMALS EMERGE FROM THE

ls emerge from the

DRY SAND AND T

y sand and

ROXIMATELY

proximately

CRAWL TO T

d crawl to

IS THOUSAND

is thousand

A I T

Donny and a few
friends from AIT took
the trip from Ft. Gordon
to Daytona Beach the
summer of 1993. Even
though he doesn't keep
in touch, he still has
the memories that
will last a lifetime.

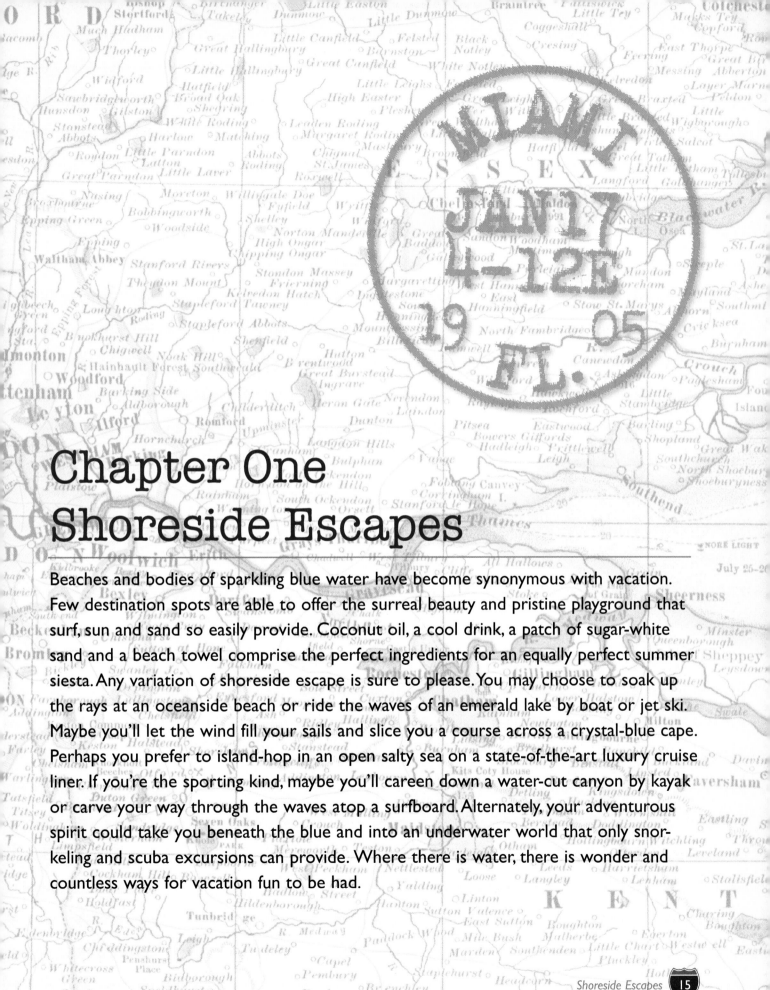

Chapter One
Shoreside Escapes

Beaches and bodies of sparkling blue water have become synonymous with vacation. Few destination spots are able to offer the surreal beauty and pristine playground that surf, sun and sand so easily provide. Coconut oil, a cool drink, a patch of sugar-white sand and a beach towel comprise the perfect ingredients for an equally perfect summer siesta. Any variation of shoreside escape is sure to please. You may choose to soak up the rays at an oceanside beach or ride the waves of an emerald lake by boat or jet ski. Maybe you'll let the wind fill your sails and slice you a course across a crystal-blue cape. Perhaps you prefer to island-hop in an open salty sea on a state-of-the-art luxury cruise liner. If you're the sporting kind, maybe you'll careen down a water-cut canyon by kayak or carve your way through the waves atop a surfboard. Alternately, your adventurous spirit could take you beneath the blue and into an underwater world that only snorkeling and scuba excursions can provide. Where there is water, there is wonder and countless ways for vacation fun to be had.

Beach Vacation

COMBINE CIRCLES AND STRAIGHT LINES

Using circles and stripes together on a layout adds visual excitement. Cut two large half circles from cardstock (SEI); mount to opposite corners of page. Mat two photos; adhere next to opposite-colored half circles. Leave third photo unmatted. Use coordinating striped paper (SEI) to mat printed journaling block. Apply letter stickers (SEI) and hand journaling to circle tags (SEI). Adhere tags slightly over edges of page; trim. Affix striped tags (SEI) with snaps (Making Memories). To finish, add eyelet letters (Making Memories) and cut out title letters (www.twopeasinabucket.com) to coordinating striped paper (SEI); mount on page using metal snap.

Tracy Miller, Fallston, Maryland

Thank You

PUT A "TURN" ON YOUR 8½ x 11" LAYOUTS

Complete this intricate-looking layout in no time. Turn page horizontally. Tear edges from blue cardstock; crumple. Flatten and ink paper randomly with sand-colored ink on torn edges. Affix photo to seashell frame (Cloud 9 Design) matted to torn and inked tan cardstock. Repeat with journaling block (Cloud 9 Design). Print journaling and name strip onto transparencies; adhere journaling block and bottom of picture. Wrap frame in fibers, securing with concho (source unknown). To finish, add beach cut-outs (Cloud 9 Design) using self-adhesive foam spacers on a few for a 3-D effect.

Sam Cousins, Shelton, Connecticut

Beach Combers
SAVE SAND AND SHELLS IN A SHAKER BOX

Bring a little of the beach home in a shaker box. Print poem onto left page background. Mount large piece of torn brown cardstock to top of left page, and smaller piece to top of right page. Scan photo and print three copies; crop and mount to bottom of left page. Affix torn patterned vellum (Autumn Leaves) over poem on left page and photos on bottom of right page. Mount remainder of photos. Tear out printed journaling, chalk torn edges and mount. Enclose sand and seashells in a memorabilia holder (C-Thru Ruler); seal with glue. Set eyelets in holder; run cord through, tie and mount. Add letter stickers (Colorbök) for title to torn strips of vellum. Add punched vellum footprints to bottom of left page to complete.

Sheila Riddle, Elk River, Minnesota

Manzanita Beach

CREATE A PICTURE-PERFECT PAGE TITLE

Write in the sand on your next beach vacation for a unique page addition—a photo title. Mat photos using various techniques: tear and roll, double mat, etc. For title photo, leave bottom mat slightly larger; add beach cut-outs (EK Success) using self-adhesive foam spacers. Sew vellum pockets onto journaling squares; add seashell charm (Darice). Set eyelets into pages; string various fibers through eyelets, tying charms (Darice) to ends. Add matted cut-outs with self-adhesive foam spacers to fibers on right page and hang unmatted cut-outs to fibers on third page.

Tami Comstock, Pocatello, Idaho

Bahamas

GET THRIFTY WITH PAGE ADDITIONS

This unique palm tree art was acquired from the pages of a vintage book discovered at a thrift store. Position photo onto brown cardstock. Adhere coastal netting (Magic Scraps). Stamp "Bahamas" using printer-style stamp letters (Hero Arts) and black ink. To create tag, brush a manila shipping tag with walnut ink and streak with makeup wedge. Cut out vintage book art and adhere to tag with decoupage adhesive; age edges with sepia ink. Coat entire surface of tag with decoupage adhesive; attach fibers. Stamp "beach" onto transparency and affix with brown eyelets. Adhere tag to page. String fibers across top of cardstock; embellish with seashells (U.S. Shell) affixed with glue dots. Stamp sand pattern (Club Scrap) across bottom of cardstock with sepia ink. Complete by inking edges with sepia ink.

Jlyne Hanback, Biloxi, Mississippi

My First Ocean Swim

PAINT A TRANSPARENCY

Many scrapbookers print journaling onto transparencies—now try painting on them! Tear a rectangle section from patterned cardstock (source unknown); adhere at a slant onto yellow background. Print title and journaling onto transparency; tear out and adhere with silver eyelets. Use one part brown acrylic paint (Delta) to six parts liquid adhesive; apply to rectangle transparency and cut out center to make frame. Mount frame over picture with eyelets. String beads with wire and hang from eyelets.

Jlyne Hanback, Biloxi, Mississippi

A Boy At The Beach

TAG YOUR TITLES

Use a template to make tags for your title for an eye-pleasing page addition. Begin by printing part of title and journaling onto vellum; tear out and adhere to background page. Tear strips from blue vellum; mount long strip to upper part of page and small strip at bottom of journaling. Add small punched photos and swirl clip to small strip. Mount photos. Using tag template (Deluxe Designs), make two tags for part of title. Add embossing powder to edges of first letter tag. Using lettering template, punches, stencils or stamps and a round tool, create title as shown. Add chalk and fibers for detail. Mount on page. Create embellishments by covering a cardboard medallion with extra thick embossing powder and sand-colored embossing powder. While enamel is still hot, press inked stamp (Hero Arts) into enamel to make an impression. Adhere to torn vellum piece on top of fibers. Add swirl clip to finish.

Valerie Barton, Flowood, Mississippi

Cousins Make The Best Friends

GIVE YOUR BEACH LAYOUT A REALISTIC FEEL

Use actual sea shells for a realistic effect on your beach pages. Tear out the center of two sheets of beach patterned paper (Wübie Prints), creating a frame when pages are placed together. Adhere blue paterned paper (Creative Imaginations) beneath. Trim edges and mount on black cardstock. Mount coastal netting to left page as border, and to right page corners. Mat photos on back of ocean printed paper (Provo Craft); tear and roll torn sections of mat towards photo, exposing print; affix to page. Remove the center of circle tags. Add gold embossing powder to edges. Replace center with water patterned paper (Wübie Prints) that has been printed with journal words. Add embellished water tags, seashells, starfish and seahorse (U.S. Shell Inc). Print title onto transparency, sprinkle with embossing powder and heat to set. Mount mica sheets (USArtQuest) atop transparencies with brads. Add several layers of extra thick embossing powder and corners of mica tiles; add shells and beads to hot enamel on the last layer to embellish. Make envelope from shell vellum (Autumn Leaves); set eyelets. Lace with paper yarn (Making Memories); hang charms (Boutique Trims) and wrapped wire. Print journaling onto paper; cut out, chalk and slip into envelope. Add seashells.

Denise Tucker, Versailles, Indiana

Paradise

CREATE A "CHARMING" TROPICAL TAG

A fun way to display a charming photo is next to a charming tag. Tear patterned paper (NRN Designs) diagonally; mount to background paper (NRN Designs). Mat photos to white cardstock. Double mat focal photo to patterned paper (NRN Designs). Cut out first word in title; adhere. Print journaling onto patterned paper and tear at bottom; add sticker letters (NRN Designs), beads and shell die cuts (NRN Designs). Mount fabric scraps to bottom left corner. Make tag using stickers and die cuts. Finish with fibers, beads (All The Extras) and charms (All The Extras).

Susan Stringfellow, Cypress, Texas

Crisp And Cool

GIVE YOUR PAGE ADDED PUNCH WITH PRE-MADE TAGS

Pre-made page embellishments are a great way to construct a quick and easy layout. Cut two photos into random sections; adhere to page. Mat and mount top right photo; add seashell corners (EK Success). Tear sections from patterned paper (source unknown); mat to cardstock. Tear and roll edges back slightly; adhere to page at corners and middle. Add pre-made tags (EK Success) with brads. Apply title to sliced photo with letter phrase (EK Success). Handwrite onto vellum strip; attach with brads.

Julie Roanoke, Las Vegas, Nevada

Love

ADD FIBERS FOR A FINISHING TOUCH

Pull colors from your photos to make interesting photo mats. Print journaling directly onto cardstock. Cut patterned paper (Colors By Design) in "L" shape; mount to cardstock background (Bazzill). Print journaling directly onto cardstock. Mat photo offset onto corrugated paper. Tie fibers around right edge. Adhere scrap strip of corrugated paper tied with fibers diagonally across photo corner. Punch 1" square from a 2" square of light blue velvet paper. Tie fibers around opposite corners; mount over small photo. To finish, add title and square stickers (Creative Imaginations).

Sahily Gonzalez, Miami, Florida

*Marco Island was our first vacation ever,
and to this date it still is our favorite place to visit.
The days there are just beautiful
and good Friday was not exception.
It was hot but there was a nice breeze
which kept the temperature just perfect.
We couldn't stay the night, but it doesn't matter
because I know this won't be the last time we go.*

My Hope For You

**SHOWCASE SPECIAL MOMENTS
WITH SLIDE MOUNTS**

Use an enlarged photo with special journaling to convey meaningful sentiments. Tear top of green cardstock and strip from patterned sand paper (Creative Imaginations); mount both to background. Scan photo to enlarge; print onto white cardstock in grayscale. Affix printed journaling atop photo; adhere. Use slide mounts to hold shells and beads by placing pieces of clear acetate on both front and back of opening and adhering together with shells and beads enclosed inside. Use another a slide mount to frame a smaller photo. Affix to page. Apply date with letter stamps (Hero Arts). Freehand cut title using craft knife and adhere.

Lisa Dixon, East Brunswick, New Jersey

Beachn

CREATE BEADED PHOTO BORDERS

Use interesting items like cheesecloth for special effects. Mount spattered art-mesh (Club Scrap) onto paper (Club Scrap). Brush brown ink over entire torn piece of sand-colored cardstock and adhere to bottom of page. Affix top photo. Add title with alphabet tile stickers (Making Memories) and brads (Creative Imaginations) decorated with letter stickers. Use a tag sticker (Creative Imaginations) on tag and mount with decorated brad. Apply glue around edge of cropped photos; apply a thin layer of micro beads; mount to page. Ink edges of definitions (Making Memories) and mount. Adhere micro beads to cheesecloth; mount diagonally along torn edge of cardstock.

Sam Cousins, Shelton, Connecticut

The Oregon Coast
WEAVE A BACKGROUND PAGE

Add texture and dimension to a page by weaving a background. For left side, begin with 1" strips of cardstock. Weave together strips, gluing ends to edge strip as you go. Double mat photo to various torn sections of vellum and a patterned paper mat (Keeping Memories Alive). Adhere with wire, securing on front and back with twists. Write title onto torn vellum strip; mat and adhere with wire. For right page, mat photo to extra-large patterned paper mat. Cover with vellum, cutting rectangle section to frame photo through opening. Tear section from lower part of mat; attach two sections with wire, twisting at various spots as desired; adhere to page. Journal on mat. Weave vertical section for border, this time using patterned paper in center. Mat and adhere over torn vellum pieces. Add photos to finish.

Melissa Pilakowski, Sparks, Nebraska

Sunkissed

USE VISUAL VARIETY FOR
EYE-CATCHING COMPOSITION

To make a layout more interesting, use variety on your page. Ink edges of background paper, faded panoramic photo and cropped photos. Print journaling on transparencies. Mount photos, ribbon, and journaling, adding charm to ribbon. Add title using a variety of letter stickers (Doodlebug Design, Making Memories, Foofala, Creative Imaginations, EK Success) and inked definition stickers (Making Memories) throughout pages. Use brads where desired. Download sun from Internet (www.twopeasinabucket.com); print on transparency. Cut out, color, and adhere with spray adhesive (Creative Imaginations). Finish by adding subtitles with various additional stickers.

Sam Cousins, Shelton, Connecticut

Conch Hunters

DISGUISE JOURNALING BENEATH PHOTOS

Use many photos and tell a story all on one layout. Chalk and punch holes around entire edge of page. String jute through holes; tie off at top and bottom. Cut two 8½ x 3½" strips of cardstock; fold in half. Stamp seashell (Inkadinkado) onto journaling paper and folded cardstock. Adhere printed journaling inside. Affix jute to each side of opening. Add matted photos; mount to page. Freehand cut title and adhere to outside cover. To complete, mat focal photo and adhere. Tie journaling flaps together.

Barb DeShaw, Short Hills, New Jersey

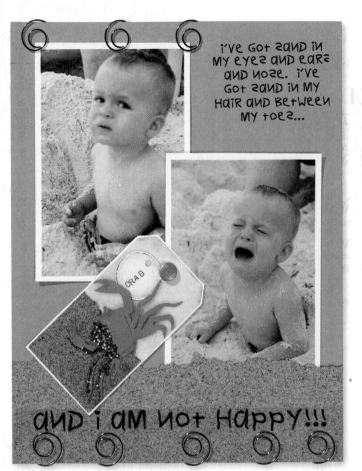

i've got sand in my eyes and ears and nose. i've got sand in my hair and between my toes...

CRAB

and i am not happy!!!

And I Am Not Happy

CAPTURE EVEN THOSE NOT-SO-HAPPY MOMENTS

Use "childish" fonts to make a striking impact and to play up a little one's lost temper! Print journaling onto background page. Tear strip from cork (Magic Scraps) for border; mount to page. Print title onto transparency and mount to cork with swirl clips. Adhere photos, tucking one behind the cork. Add swirl clips to top for embellishment. Add tag (Li'l Davis) with brad that has been heat embossed with red embossing powder.

Sam Cousins, Shelton, Connecticut

Beauty And The Beach

USE CORKBOARDS FOR PINUPS

Decorate slide holders to look like mini frames. Mount 8½ x 11" cork sheet to 12 x 12" background paper. Print title, mat on white cardstock; adhere to page. Mount 1½" cut photos to paper strip. Cover with sticker-adorned (EK Success) slide holders; mount strip to cork. Double mat photo, leaving length at end for printed caption and fibers. Affix decorated slide over desired area of picture. Print journaling onto vellum: mount to cork. Embellish with 3-D stickers (EK Success).

Angela Marvel, Puyallup, Washington

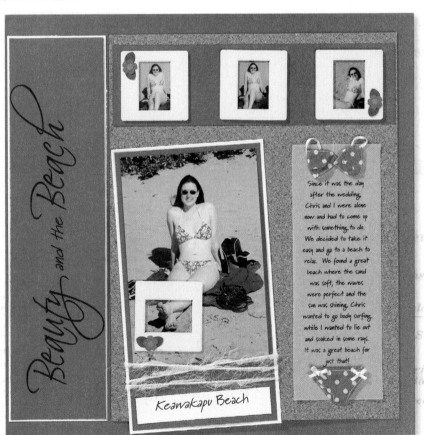

Beauty and the Beach

Since it was the day after the wedding, Chris and I were alone now and had to come up with something to do. We decided to take it easy and go to a beach to relax. We found a great beach where the sand was soft, the waves were perfect and the sun was shining. Chris wanted to go body surfing while I wanted to lie out and soaked in some rays. It was a great beach for just that!

Keawakapu Beach

Waimanalo

BLEND PHOTOS WITH POSTCARDS

Use a simple design to keep the focus on beautiful photos and picture postcards. For left page, mat photos with eyelets on patterned vellum (EK Success); tear off bottom edge. Print journaling onto transparency; adhere to page. Using craft knife, cut out title letters using font (www.twopeasinabucket.com) as a guide; adhere. For right page, double mat top photo to patterned vellum and cardstock; adhere to page with eyelets. To finish, mount remaining photos and postcards.

Heidi Dillon, Salt Lake City, Utah

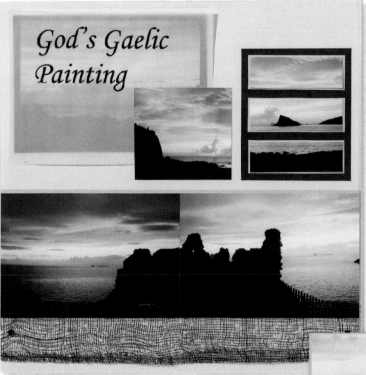

God's Gaelic Painting

CAPTURE THE COLORS OF YOUR PHOTOS WITH FIBERS

Pull all the colors that are in your photos from your fiber bag to add texture and color to a layout. Crop and mat photos with single and double mats; mount on page. Mount coastal netting (Magic Scraps) at bottom of right and left pages; add brads at ends. Print title and journaling onto vellum. Mount title on top of photo on left page and journaling onto right page. Crumple a 3¾ x 5" piece of black cardstock. Flatten and iron cardstock. Add slits to right and left sides. Wrap fibers around and through slits and adhere to black cardstock. To complete, mat and adhere to right page.

Valerie Barton, Flowood, Mississippi
Photos: Willard Gray, Jackson, Mississippi

Through the window I beheld the spectral castle, the sea upon which the light was dying, the purple fringe of Harris on the horizon and seated here in the remotest corner of Skye, amongst people whom I have never seen, girt by walls of cliffs and the sounding sea, in a region too in which there was no proper night, I confess to have been conscious of a pleasant feeling of strangeness, of removal from all customary conditions of thought and locality, which I like at times to recall and enjoy over again.

~Alexander Smith
"A Summer in Skye 1865"

Caribbean Blue

USE WAVE PATTERNED PAPER FOR MOVEMENT

The waves and colors in this layout create a breezy feel to complement the cruise theme. Adhere a wide strip of green paper (Karen Foster Design) across both pages. Tear wavy strips of striped paper (Paper Adventures); mount horizontally on top of left page, vertically on right page and across bottom where pages meet. Mat photos on white cardstock; use corner punch (Carl) on corners. Double mat photo on bottom right, placing wavy tear under photo. Print and tear out journaling; adhere over torn wave paper. Cut title (QuicKutz) from blue patterned paper (Sandylion); double mat, winding thread through letters; mount. Apply rub-on words (Making Memories). Wrap metal plaques (Making Memories) with fibers, knotting in front. Mount to page with self-adhesive foam spacers. Add knotted fiber to title. Finish by adhering beads randomly around page using crystal lacquer (Ranger).

Torrey Miller, Thornton, Colorado
Photos: Heidi Finger, Brighton, Colorado

Disney Magic

CRAFT AN INTRICATE DESIGN

Kelli creates a detailed title by combining punched pieces, die-cut lettering and intricate craft knife cutting. Use a decorative corner punch on a double mat for top right photo; adhere to background page with unmatted photos. Computer print journaling to same color cardstock; cut out, frame and mount to bottom of page. Use various border and corner punches (Family Treasures, McGill, All Night Media, Punch Bunch) to create the title frame. Die-cut "Magic" (QuicKutz) and cut out "Disney" with a craft knife; adhere. Add additional punched pieces to form the Mickey head design.

Kelli Noto, Centennial, Colorado

The Disney Magic is an awesome boat! We were onboard for a whole week and still didn't see it all.

*950 staff members
*11 passenger decks
*15,000 square feet of children's areas
*6 restaurants
*3 pools
*2 theatres
*8 lounges
*non-stop FUN!

Cruising Alaska

PRINT PICTURES ON VELLUM

Achieve a subtle backdrop with an enlarged photo printed onto vellum to create the look of a store-bought patterned paper. Select photo and enlarge to size of background page; print onto vellum. Add title and journaling to picture by sending through printer again, or by using photo-editing software. Mat on white cardstock. Print title and journaling onto it and mount to page. Add scrapbook nails (Chatterbox) to corners. Use lettering template (C-Thru Ruler) to crop letters from photos; mat to white cardstock. Adhere to page with self-adhesive foam spacers.

Trudy Sigurdson, Victoria, British Columbia, Canada
Photos: Phyllis Wright, Victoria, British Columbia, Canada

Snapshots Of Cozumel

INCORPORATE A VARIETY OF TEXTURES

Using many textures adds instant visual appeal. Trim 1/8" from edges of light blue paper. Crumple, flatten, iron and sew onto background page. Mount double sided tape, (Magic Scraps) to 2 x 7" strip of cardstock. Weave raffia strips together and adhere with double-sided tape to form title background. Trim off excess from edges. Add eyelets and knotted twine to corners. Create title using letter stickers (Me & My Big Ideas). Tear strips of sandpaper for bottom border; adhere with self-adhesive foam spacers. Add seashells. Stamp onto photos with letter stamps (PSX Design) and mount to page. Assemble palm tree using glitter covered, enlarged die-cut leaves (Sizzix). Create trunk with chalked, enlarged grass punches (EK Success). Finish with buttons for "coconuts" and stamp date in right corner (Making Memories).

Trudy Sigurdson, Victoria, British Columbia, Canada
Photos: Phyllis Wright, Victoria, British Columbia, Canada

Unfurl
The Sail

CREATE A BOLD GRAPHIC LOOK

Keep true to a nautical-inspired layout by mimicking the bold lines and bright colors of sails and flags. Trim two 4½" sections diagonally from blue cardstock, and one 4½" section from yellow; mount to white background paper, leaving the white corners exposed. Adhere same-colored mesh (Magenta) to each section. Mount photos. Print journaling on transparency; mount to page.

Kelli Noto, Centennial, Colorado

Tall Ships
Liberty

CREATE AN AGED LOOK

Use metallic rub-ons to give your layout an aged feel. Apply metallic rub-ons (Craf-T) around torn edges of patterned paper (Karen Foster Design). Rub blade of scissors along edge of some pictures. Apply metallic rub-ons to edges. Color copy the die-cut ship to a patina color; wet, crumple, tear edges and apply walnut ink. Apply letter stickers (Colorbök) to torn vellum. Use rub-ons to age edges and adhere over die-cut ship. Add ribbons (Making Memories) and message bottle (7 Gypsies) filled with micro beads beads and sand attached to eyelet with hemp string. Mount two tags that have been crumpled and aged with walnut ink together with hinges. Add journaling, map scraps and other photo to inside; embellish outside with nautical ephemera. Attach label holder (Magic Scraps) to top of tag. Add mesh scrap (Making Memories), faux wax seal (Creative Imaginations) and poem stone sentiment (Creative Imaginations).

Diana Graham, Barrington, Illinois

Kayakin'

CREATE BALANCE WITH A MOSAIC BORDER

Combine brightly colored mosaics and mesh for instant added flair. Attach green patterned paper (NRN Designs) to blue background. Adhere mesh paper (Magenta) at an angle halfway off page. Trim excess around edges. Add mosaic tiles (Magic Scraps) randomly. Mount matted photos. Use lettering template to create letters. Apply three layers of extra thick embossing powder; mount to mesh. Write journaling on blue cardstock shape and repeat embossing technique; mount. Sew embroidery floss (DMC) around the edges of page and mesh paper.

Shannon Taylor, Bristol, Tennessee

Sailing The San Juan Islands

USE FABRIC IN A BACKGROUND

Applying a cheesecloth background gives this layout a coastal feel. Sew fabric onto background paper. Enlarge photo. Wrap hemp around left edge of photo; tie off, adding beads and charms (source unknown). Use large letter stamps (Wordsworth) on shapes cut from handmade paper for title; ink corners. Ink edges of an additional handmade paper square for bead and charm embellishments. Stamp (PSX Design) words onto photo. Ink edges of paper strips. Place journaling printed onto transparencies on top. Mount with brads on one end and twine on the other. Finish by embellishing with beads and charms (source unknown).

Trudy Sigurdson, Victoria, British Columbia, Canada

Wet 'N' Wild

MIMIC A WATER EFFECT

Put a splash in your title! Cut two 4¼ x 11½" sections from yellow cardstock; mount to orange background. Adhere photos onto sections. Using wave patterned scissors (Fiskars), cut blue cardstock strips; mount over photos, allowing yellow to peek through bottom. Crop two photos into tag shapes; set eyelets into top. Attach string; hang from blue wave strip on right page with brad. Adhere remaining photos. Print journaling; cut top with wavy scissors; mount. Use circles punched from yellow cardstock and ¼" strips to affix to page and photos. Using flip option in word processing program, print title words on cardstock. Use scissors and craft knife to cut title. Freehand cut splash droplets; add crystal lacquer (JudiKins) for water effect. Mount to page.

Natalie Abbott, Lakewood, Colorado
Photos: Sue Romsos, Cameron, Wisconsin

Cold Creek Adventure

CREATE DIMENSION WITH MODELING PASTE

When combined, modeling paste and paint make a fun page addition, as well as an artistic means for re-creating water. Mat patterned paper (source unknown) on cardstock background. Double mat top photo, tearing mats' left sides. Make photo tags with torn and chalked bottom edges; print journaling onto vellum tag; attach on top of photo tags with large brad. Embellish title tag with tree stickers (Sandylion), mesh and letter stickers (Creative Imaginations); adhere with foam squares. Affix large photo onto page. Cut foam core board into corner piece; adhere cardstock atop and tear along cut edge of board; chalk all edges. Use rock stickers (Creative Imaginations) and tree stickers with foam squares for dimension. Mix blue acrylic paint (Delta) into modeling paste (USArtQuest) and apply with a small spatula, giving it a wave-like texture, adding darker colors on the bottom. Cut 1" squares from board; mount photos underneath; adhere to page.

Kelly Angard, Highlands Ranch, Colorado

Sunset Surf

COLOR TISSUE PAPER LETTERS

Tissue paper is perfect for chalking since it absorbs color so well. Adhere tissue to white cardstock; cut letters using craft knife and template (Scrap Pagerz); chalk and mount. Tear several sections from different colored cardstocks, including a few wave patterns. Chalk edges and mount to background page. Tear photos and adhere. Print journaling onto vellum. Tear out and chalk; mount to page. Apply liquid adhesive (Suze Weinberg) to edge of wave and apply large micro beads (Halcraft).

Pam Canavan, Clermont, Florida

Laguna Beach

"NAIL" A TITLE

Use nailheads on a strip to create a sharp-looking page title. First, cut a 3½ x 7" section from water patterned paper (Wordsworth). Mount to black cardstock background (Bazzill). Print journaling to 4¾ x 8½" section of white cardstock; adhere on right. Mat 5 x 7" photo; affix to page. Mount labels (Dymo). Attach letter nailheads (Scrapworks) to white cardstock strip; mount. Adhere remaining photos. Repeat water patterned paper in bottom corner.

Diana Hudson, Bakersfield, California
Photos: Mona Shield Payne, Henderson, Nevada

Speed

EMBELLISH SLIDE MOUNTS

Use clear embossing powders to add instant shine to your embellishments. Mat patterned paper (Karen Foster Design) on turquoise and blue cardstock. Using an embossing pen, outline wave details on paper. Heat emboss extra thick embossing powder mixed with blue glitter on details. Touch slide mounts (Hot Off The Press) to both blue and turquoise ink pads until desired color is achieved. Add several layers of mixed powder to slide mounts, heating in between layers. Mount small photos behind smaller slide mounts. Mat with inked white cardstock. Mount on page. Mat large photo in the same fashion. Add larger slide mount over detail of picture. Die-cut letters (QuicKutz) and emboss in the same technique as slide mounts. Adhere to torn, inked white circles and add to page. Affix journaling printed on transparency. Finish by embossing paper clips (Making Memories) and add to page.

Jodi Amidei, Memory Makers Books
Photos: Bruce Aldridge, Broomfield, Colorado

Wave Riders

MAKE DIMENSIONAL WAVES

Layer a variety of papers for a wave-inspired look. Attach torn layers with rolled edges on bottom and upper left corner of page. Print journaling, cut and tear out; chalk. String beads (JewelCraft) onto blue wire; attach to journaling; mount with self-adhesive foam spacers. Cut letters from corrugated paper for first part of title; stamp letters (Wordsworth) and emboss second part of title. Use dimensional glue (Plaid) to make water droplets and stripes. Mat photos; mount using self-adhesive foam spacers. Add striped paper clips (Staples) and cut-out word and add to upper photo and wax seals (Creative Imaginations) to bottom photos. Print onto chalked tag. Using small letter stamps (PSX Design), stamp names above photos and date onto tag. Tie fibers onto tag; mount, tucking behind top wave photo.

Holle Wiktorek, Reunion, Colorado

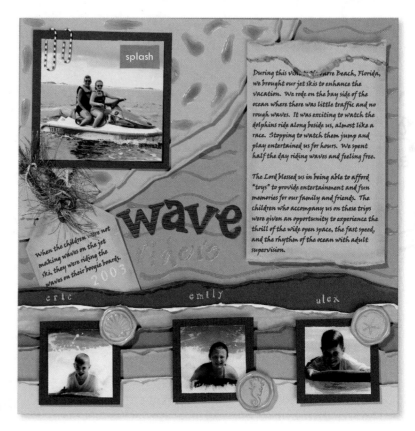

H2OH!

INCORPORATE HANDMADE PAPER FOR TEXTURE

Use a variety of textures for added interest. Cut 4¾ x 11½" section from water patterned paper (Wübie Prints); mount to bottom of handmade paper (Artistic Scrapper). Mount mesh (Magic Scraps) along top. Using stamps (Hero Arts), stamp "just" onto vellum and apply letter stickers (Wordsworth) for "ski." Highlight stickers with dimensional glue (Plaid). Double mat, first on crumpled dark blue cardstock, then on light blue; adhere with brads along with photos. Print journaling onto vellum; tear out. Highlight desired words with chalk and dimensional glue (Plaid); ink torn edges with blue ink. Mat last photo to mulberry; add brads for embellishments. Adhere metal letters (Scrapyard 329) to tile squares (EK Success) matted on mulberry. Mix with sticker letters (Wordsworth) highlighted with dimensional glue.

Holle Wiktorek, Reunion, Colorado

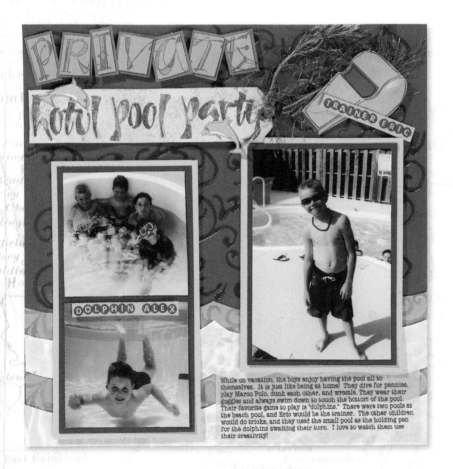

Private Hotel Pool Party

STAMP A DIMENSIONAL BACKGROUND

Create a raised look to your background without embossing. First, stamp background page with scroll stamp (Hero Arts). Outline with dimensional glue (Plaid). Stamp scroll onto section of wave-cut light blue paper for bottom border; highlight with silver pen. Mount two strips of sanded wave-cut water paper. Print journaling onto blue vellum; attach at bottom. Double mat photos, mounting two on vertical mat. Use alphabet stamps (PSX Design) for photo captions. Mount matted photos and laser whistle die (Li'l Davis) with self-adhesive foam spacers. Stamp letters (Wordsworth) for first part of title; cut out each letter; mat and mount with self-adhesive foam spacers. Stamp (Wordsworth) second part of title; outline with dimensional glue and add highlights with pen. Cut second part of title into tag shape; add eyelet and fibers and mount with self-adhesive foam spacers. Complete by adding dolphin stickers (EK Success).

Holle Wiktorek, Reunion, Colorado

Snorkeling Molokini

CROP TO MAXIMIZE SPACE

Underwater photos are perfect for cropping…especially when you want to keep the focus on certain elements. Begin by cropping top off patterned paper (Making Memories); adhere to bottom of right and left pages. Mount photos and vellum journaling blocks to pages with eyelets. Crop photos for top of pages using a square punch and freehand cutting. Use letter punches (QuicKutz) for title.

Heidi Dillon, Salt Lake City, Utah
Photos: Daniel Steenblik, Salt Lake City, Utah

Snorkeling

FORM FRAMES WITH TEARING AND BEADS

Spice up your photo mats with bead borders. Mat a 4" strip of patterned paper (Paper Adventures) with white torn cardstock. Roll torn edges and mount along bottom. Punch out, mat and adhere three small photos to water paper. Secure string of beads (JewelCraft) at top and bottom of section from behind with tape. Mat focal photo with torn white cardstock. Roll torn edges and apply glue; cover with micro beads (Halcraft). Print title and journaling onto vellum; mount to page. Affix small strip of water paper across journaling block and behind focal photo. Add small punched squares to bottom corners. To finish, add title (Creative Imaginations) and frame (Making Memories).

Valerie Barton, Flowood, Mississippi

Grenada Spice Island

GET CREATIVE WITH STAMPING

Try this fun stamping technique. Tear a small corner section from tan cardstock; stamp with texture stamp (Club Scrap) using clear embossing ink and embossing powder; heat to set. Restamp with metallic copper ink over embossed area. Adhere to page. Use self-adhesive letter stickers (Creative Imaginations) on brads for title. Punch square from corner of blue patterned paper (Club Scrap). Attach small sunset photo behind square. Adhere to background paper. Adhere coastal netting to bottom corner and one top corner. Use sand dollar stamp (Club Scrap) on mica tiles (USArtQuest); adhere to page. Affix matted and enlarged photo. For tag and journaling, use reed stamp (Club Scrap) masked off at tips. Ink and stamp with light green ink. Remove masking tape, mask off areas just inked and ink tips with darker green ink; stamp page. Finish by tying off tag; add starfish (Bag Of Beach); mount beads (Halcraft) to torn strip and adhere to journaling box with foam tape.

Michelle Pesce, Arvada, Colorado

Snorkeling

FIND ADDITIONAL USES
FOR OFFICE SUPPLIES

Clips, staples and tags make for outstanding page embellishments. Mat tan cardstock on blue cardstock. Attach mesh (Magenta) to bottom corner with colored staples (Staples). Punch printed words (KI Memories) into circles and adhere to tags. Mat photos and adhere to page, using brads and staples where desired. Add patterned paper (KI Memories) to top corner before attaching final photo. Make preprinted slide mount into a shakerbox by covering hole with acetate, filling with sand and shells (Magic Scraps) and adhering to blue cardstock square. Embellish page with preprinted words mounted on tags (Making Memories) with floss-tied tags using self-adhesive foam spacers. Add postcard with white frame highlight and word to complete page.

Diana Graham, Barrington, Illinois

from the Master's Hand....

Paradise!

The beauty and wonder of nature has always been a huge part of my life. My parents started taking me to the mountains at a very early age. We hiked, camped, backpacked, white-water rafted and just enjoyed quick day trips to get a way from the hustle of everyday life in the city. I will always thank my mother and father for the respect I have now as an adult for the outdoors. It wasn't until Tom brought this particular picture home that I realized why he must enjoy his annual hunting trip so much. The beauty all around him is so striking, but more than that, I believe this must also be a time of deep reflection for him. When you are in such a vast expanse of Gods creation, you gain perspective on your life. Suddenly you realize that you are but a small, small part of this world and your troubles don't seem near as important. You gain appreciation for the comforts we take for granted, and problems just seem to lift off your shoulders. Someday I hope to travel to this spot with Tom, but for now I appreciate the revitalizing effect it has on his precious soul, and I thank God each time he returns safely home.

paradise found!

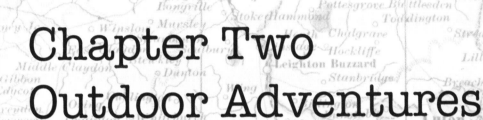

Chapter Two
Outdoor Adventures

Vacations needn't include five-star accommodations to be first-rate travel experiences. While resorts and room service have their perks, nature and the great wide open offer unparalleled accommodations when what you are seeking is a stunning view and access to entertainment and activity. Crisp clean air, quiet serenity and inherent peacefulness leave many an exclusive spa in wanting of what outdoor adventures so effortlessly provide. You may choose to venture into the wild frontier on a road trip or weave your way up a rugged mountainside trail. Maybe you'll watch in wonder from behind the curtain of a rushing waterfall or skillfully pick your steps to reach a lofty sheer-sided summit. Perhaps you'd prefer to retreat to a rustic log cabin haven beside a trout-wealthy lake. Or maybe you'll opt to explore a forgotten cavern, set up camp in the heart of a forest or play on white powdered slopes with skis and snowmobiles. No matter the majestic backdrop, any outdoor excursion will make for a peak vacation experience.

Road Rules for

You must have long range walkie-talkies for proper communication between cars. Let Harley, Dylan & Sarah say 'Come in Candy Cane' at least once every 10 miles

Have an old map for Good Luck. Forget the fact that the roads have expanded and changed over the years, and get lost within 50 miles from home.

Getting There

MARY our Driver

Take the back roads whenever possible. They are virtually deserted, lacking proper rest stops, subject to detours and filled with interesting sites.

Have two car loads of people. Three adults, Three pre-teens and one 9 month old. Stop often for food, washroom breaks, map deciphering and diaper changes.

HARLEY + GRACE

Make sure your map reader knows what she is doing. Sometimes, there are two roads with the same number, and the difference is in the direction. For example Road 121 North or 121 South.

Have lots of fun laughing your heads off at stupid signs, silly songs the kids sing, speed limits, strange towns and jokes shared between the two cars.

Behind us are Nancy, Sarah & Dylan

Road Rules For Getting There

JOURNAL YOUR ROAD TRIP

Jot down all your fun and silly memories from your trip to use in your layout. Mat map patterned paper (source unknown) to blue background pages. Double mat photos, making larger mats for main photo on left page. Stamp date onto vellum mat. Set eyelet above date. Distress and chalk small tag (2DYE4); add journaling. Tie with floss (DMC) to key chain, add key, and hang from eyelet. Set eyelets into photo on right page; hang distressed tag through eyelets with twisted floss. Make a copy of photo with car following in rear windshield. Punch out car and mat on blue cardstock. Attach third tag to back of punched car. Line up to original photo and mount with self-adhesive foam spacers. Print journaling onto vellum; cut out. Tear off tops and bottoms; chalk edges and stitch to pages. Print title onto cardstock; mat and mount with self-adhesive foam spacers.

Ruth De Fauw, Woodstock, Ontario, Canada

Journey 2003

COMBINE RUB-ONS AND COMPUTER JOURNALING

Keep layouts clean and balanced with straight lines and coordinating colors. Cut a 4½" strip and a 7" strip from 12 x 12" light gray paper (SEI). Print journaling onto both sections; mount smaller section to dark yellow background and larger section to dark gray background. Mat shot of dashboard to strip on left page, leaving room for letter stickers (EK Success); apply stickers. Mount all photos. Cut ½" strips from dark gray and yellow papers. Adhere to bottom of page, leaving space to mount definitions (Colorbök). Add star brads. Use tags (Colorbök) and additional definitions to embellish page. Apply rub-ons (Making Memories). Attach final picture with letter stickers under gray paper.

Renae Clark, Mazomanie, Wisconsin

Are We There Yet?

CAPTURE THE QUIETER MOMENTS

Emboss the edge of a photo for a unique added touch. Stamp title onto cardstock and inked circle tag with various letter stamps (Hero Arts). Tear out title; heat emboss top tom edge with blue embossing powder. Set eyelets into title strip. Hang title tag, tag with punched photo, and altered embossed tag from title strip. Mount tom sections of cardstocks to patterned paper (PSX Design); affix title strip. Mat photos; tear right side of mat for vertical photo; chalk and adhere to page, tucking under title tag (Making Memories). Heat emboss frame and edge of other photo; mount to page. Add fabric-covered buttons and torn embellished corner. To complete page, tie hemp string across bottom of page, wrapping several times.

Valerie Barton, Flowood, Mississippi

The Character Of A Man

FOCUS ON A SINGLE GREAT PHOTO

Nothing makes a layout more impressive than an impressive photo. Enlarge photo to 7½ x 10" and adhere to dark green cardstock. Print title onto 2" strip of light green paper. Use compass stamp (Stampabilities) on title block; mount to top of page. Stamp half compasses onto a smaller strip for bottom border; adhere to page.

Margert Ann Kruljac, Newnan, Georgia
Photo: Christopher Kruljac, Phoenixville, Pennsylvania

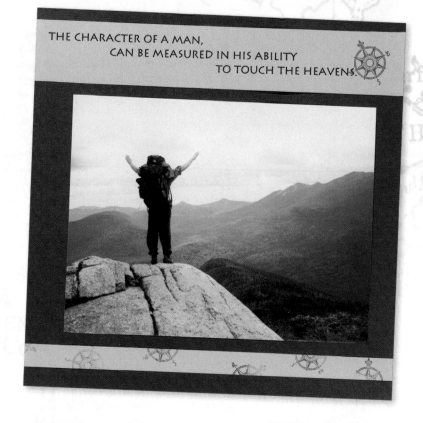

THE CHARACTER OF A MAN,
CAN BE MEASURED IN HIS ABILITY
TO TOUCH THE HEAVENS.

GOING TO THE SUN

Nature Walk

Going To The Sun

CAPTURE BEAUTIFUL SCENERY

Use natural elements in pages celebrating the great outdoors. Apply strip of mesh (Pulsar) across top of left and bottom of right natural-hued background papers. Print journaling, mat along with remaining photos and mount. Add pre-made accent tags (EK Success) and embellishments. Use square punch (Marvy/Uchida) to punch out part of photo; adhere to page with self-adhesive foam spacers. Add title with letter stamps (Rubber Stampede) in green ink. Stack-mat three photos horizontally on left page and vertically on right. Adhere to pages.

Julia Moncrief, Lakeside, Montana

A MAN WHO IS TRUSTING IN HIS FAITH
KNOWS IN HIS HEART,
THAT JUST BEYOND THE MIST
LIES SOMETHING MAJESTIC.

A Man Who Is Trusting...

PRINT ON AN ENLARGED PHOTO

You don't always have to put your title or journaling on paper—try it right on the photo! Using photo-editing software, place title onto desired area of photo. Enlarge photo to 7½ x 10" and print. Glue fibers around edges of photo; affix to patterned paper (The Paper Loft). Cut two 1" strips from red cardstock. Mount one vertically to left side, trim other to 9" long; adhere below photo and affix fiber to centers. Double mat charms (source unknown) to torn cardstock squares; adhere to page.

Margert Ann Kruljac, Newnan, Georgia
Photo: Christopher Kruljac, Phoenixville, Pennsylvania

Nothing But Blue Skies

USE MESH AND INK TO CREATE TEXTURE

Use this technique to give your tag some texture. Adhere a section of white mesh paper (Magenta) vertically to your background page. Mount strips of cardstock covered with blue mesh (Magenta) onto page with brads. Print journaling. Cut and lightly ink edges with blue ink; adhere with brads. Mount matted photos. Print part of title onto tag. Lay mesh onto tag; lightly tap mesh with blue ink pad. Remove mesh; Freehand-cut second part of title from blue cardstock. Add fibers, wire, eyelet, charms (source unknown) and word tag (Chronicle Books); mount to page.

Anne Heyen, New Fairfield, Connecticut

One of the most beautiful and breathtaking places in the world, the Grand Canyon, was on the list of places we wanted to see on our 26 day long honeymoon. When we first parked our car, we ran to the first viewing station. My heart stopped. I just could not believe what it looked like or that I was actually standing in front of it. It was one of the places I always wanted to visit and I was standing there with my husband at the beginning of our life together. It was a perfect moment. 5/99

nothing but
blue
from now

My Journey To The Deep

PRESERVE ALL THE DETAILS WITH DESCRIPTIVE JOURNALING

Including a detailed narrative of your adventures is an engaging way to record and recall travel memories. Tear brown cardstock and adhere to bottom portions of cream-colored cardstock background pages. Double mat both page's focal photos with patterned paper (Daisy D's) and brown cardstock, leaving room for photo scraps on left page. Mount definition journaling (Making Memories) to torn brown cardstock and double mat with brown and cream cardstocks; affix photo and adhere to page. Feature memorabilia matted with patterned paper (Daisy D's) inside a slide mount (Foofala) adorned with fibers. Create title with stickers (Creative Imaginations) and metal letters (Making Memories). For right page, mount double-matted photo to page; leave second photo unmatted. Computer journal on cream-colored cardstock and mat to brown cardstock. Embellish with torn brown cardstock and frame (Making Memories) featuring handwritten date.

Vikki Hall, Rogers, Arkansas

Mercer Cavern

STRAP MEMORABILIA ONTO YOUR LAYOUT

Simulate leather straps with the right color paper and brads. For left page, mat and mount focal picture. Adhere photos to background patterned paper (Karen Foster Design). Using lettering template (Accu-Cut), cut title letters and adhere. For middle page, tear black cardstock in half. Adhere photo to printed journaling block on one side, photo to the other side. Attach cardstock strips with written words randomly across brown cardstock block with brads. For right page, spray background cardstock with gold sparkle spray (Duncan). Allow time to dry. Mat photo on gray mat adorned with border punch (Fiskars) along top edge. Add patterned paper strip behind punched edge before matting on brown cardstock. Attach travel brochures to page using cardstock strips with descriptive words using brads. Stamp travel map (All Night Media) and compass (All Night Media) on various colors of cardstock. Use matted stamped patterns as page embellishments, using patterned paper strip to highlight.

Oksanna Pope, Los Gatos, California

Waterfalls Of The Columbia River George

SLIP PHOTO TAGS INTO VELLUM POCKETS

Keep the focus on the main photos by placing other photos on tags behind vellum pockets. Mat focal photos; adhere to background patterned paper (Sweetwater). Using a craft knife, freehand cut title from cardstock, matting the first part of title; adhere to pages. Cut five 3" squares. Mount slightly smaller vellum squares on top with eyelets in each corner; adhere pockets to pages. Apply cropped photos to tags (Impress Rubber Stamps). Tie tags with paper yarn (Making Memories); slide completed tags into pockets. Print journaling on vellum; attach to photo with eyelets. Add cropped photos to top of right page to complete.

Paula Wessells, Vancouver, Washington

Multnomah Falls

MOUNT PANORAMIC PHOTO VERTICALLY

Try a vertical format for a panoramic photo for an even more dramatic look. Mat photo to gold paper, then to gold matted brown patterned paper (Hot Off The Press). Adhere to tan and ivory torn vellum; roll edges. Adhere to background patterned paper (Hot Off The Press). Cut out letters (Hot Off The Press); mount, using self-adhesive foam spacers behind every other letter and chalk. Print word for bookplate (Hot Off The Press); cut out and chalk. Place under bookplate. String fiber through bookplate ends, securing fibers behind page and under matted photo. Attach with brads. Print journaling, mat on gold paper and mount to page. Heat emboss spiral clip with gold powder. Mat tag to gold paper; add paper charms (Hot Off The Press). Adhere tag with self-adhesive foam spacer. Attach fiber around each end of clip; run fiber behind tag and attach to back of page with tape. Finish page by adding remaining paper charms.

Shauna Berglund-Immel for Hot Off The Press, Canby, Oregon

Ainsworth State Park

MAXIMIZE PAGE SPACE WITHOUT A TEMPLATE

You don't need a template to get this well-balanced, space-efficient look. Attach a 3½" strip of light green cardstock to bottom of both left and right background pages. Mount all photos. Print title and captions onto light green cardstock. Cut and mount to pages. Adhere mosaic tiles (Sarah Heidt) to caption strips. Add two ½" straps with mosaics to title box. Print journaling onto vellum. Stamp leaf stamp (Back Street, Inc.) with paint (Scrapbook Diva) on journaling blocks.

Tamara Morrison, Trabuco Canyon, California

Wish We Were There

CRAFT A COLLAGE USING POSTCARDS

Get extra mileage from your postcards by using them on your scrapbook pages. Start with background paper (Design Originals). Add torn cork paper (Magic Scraps) on bottom left corner. Cut two journaling boxes from tan cardstock; chalk edges and mount to page. Hand journal within boxes. Cut slits into postcards. Slide small strips of cardstock through and mount to small punched circles matted to small squares; attach all with brad. Adhere brads to page with postcards, covering journaling. Embellish cork with used stamps, torn cardstock pieces, stamped and inked tags, letter stickers (EK Success) clips, faux-wax seal (Creative Imaginations) and hemp string. Cut paper for title box. Adhere cork to opposite corners. Use various letter stamps (Hero Arts) and inks to apply title. Add stamp embellishment and cord to title; adhere to page.

Valerie Barton, Flowood, Mississippi

Bryce Canyon

LAYER A BACKGROUND

Mimic the landscape in your photos with a layered background. Tear sections from various patterned papers (Design Originals, Karen Foster Design, Provo Craft); adhere to background page. Sew on burlap swatch at top left corner of background. Stitch a corner pocket from burlap; adhere to bottom right corner by sewing edges to page; add button accent (JHB International) and title stickers (All My Memories). Affix photos, tucking behind layers. Print journaling on vellum and heat emboss; cut and adhere to page.

Jodi Amidei, Memory Makers Books
Photos: Quentin Hammond, Arvada, Colorado

Yellowstone National Park

CREATE YOUR OWN DIE CUT

Use a craft knife to cut your own die-cut design. To form background, cut horizontal strips from patterned paper (Club Scrap) and various cardstocks (Bazzill); adhere to page. Silhouette crop photo title; attach with hemp cord. Mat photos, double matting one to patterned paper. Tear bottom, add stitched X's, ink edges, and adhere over other photo with self-adhesive foam spacers. Print journaling; stitch onto page. Use an enlarged photocopy of the title photo as a pattern to create the handcut die cut. Using a craft knife, cut the patterns out of the center, placing colored cardstock behind openings. Ink edges, write words and embellish with hemp (Pulsar). Attach to page with self-adhesive foam spacers. Finish with stitched X's to embellish page.

Jodi Amidei, Memory Makers Books

How Tall?

DISTRESSING WITH INK

Using ink on papers lends a whole new look to a layout. Attach sections of patterned paper (Scrap Ease) and script paper (Penny Black) to olive green background paper. Print title on cream-colored cardstock. Cut to mat size, tearing bottom edge below title. Add leaf stamp (Rubber Stampede) and date stamp (Making Memories). Use ink (Ranger) to age edges; mount 5 x 7" photo to prepared mat. Mount atop sewn yellow mat. Lightly sand ruler to distress; mount. Sew buttons to ruler. Add printed, inked tag (DMD) to buttons with string. Print definitions onto linen tape (Lineco). Trim and ink edges. Affix to page with staples.

Diana Hudson, Bakersfield, California

Bounty & Beauty

CREATE OLD-FASHIONED TYPEWRITER KEYS

In a few short steps, you can have the look of a nostalgic title. Trim patterned paper (Karen Foster Design); mat to black cardstock (Bazzill). For title, trim letter stickers (EK Success) to fit inside round discs (Rollabind); fill with clear lacquer (Plaid); adhere to page with self-adhesive foam spacers. String fiber above and below title with eyelets; add fish photos silhouetted and hung on jump rings to bottom fiber. Mat photos; adhere to page using self-adhesive foam spacers. Print onto transparencies; heat emboss journaling with white powder; use black powder on caption for bookplate; adhere journaling over bottom photo with brads and caption on top photo under bookplate (Making Memories). Tear strips from black cardstock to adhere on edge of small photos; use metallic rub-ons (Craf-T) for torn edge; adhere with brads. Cut a section of ruler patterned paper (7 Gypsies) to fit over focal photo. Tear top edge and ink all edges. Adhere over bottom of photo.

Denise Tucker, Versailles, Indiana
Photos: Greg Mathews, Knoxville, Illinois

Shiprock Lake

FEATURE JOURNALING ON AN OVERSIZED TAG

Put vellum envelopes and pockets to use as artful keepers of embellishments and journaling. Tear patterned paper (Provo Craft), ink torn edge with chestnut ink and mount to dark green cardstock background pages; mount horizontally to left page and vertically to right. Mat photos on patterned paper (Sandylion), again inking edges with chestnut ink. Adhere to page. Create title with computer font printed on vellum; mat with mulberry paper (Provo Craft). Embellish with button (source unknown), fibers and tags adorned with cut-outs (EK Success) matted with mulberry paper; ink edges of tags. Ink edges of vellum envelopes (source unknown) and embellish with eyelets; affix to page and insert inked cut-outs (EK Success) and tag adorned with fibers, mulberry paper and additional cut-outs. For right page, mat three photos to patterned paper. Affix vellum block to page with eyelets to create an envelope; embellish with circle tag constructed from patterned paper (Provo Craft), silver embossing powder and hat cut-out. String through eyelet with fiber. Computer journal onto oversized tag using template (Deluxe Designs); embellish with mulberry paper, cut-outs and fibers. Insert tag into vellum envelope.

Cynthia Coulon, Provo, Utah

Fishing In Mexico

ADD DIMENSION WITH A BAMBOO BORDER

Create this fun border easily. Adhere burlap to background page. Cut wooden dowels into 12" sections. Rub dowels with metallic rub-ons (Craf-T). Glue strips of raffia at intervals on dowels; when dry, rub raffia with black metallic rub-on. Tie ends together with cord and attach border to background. Cut cardboard for title box; cover with clay (Polyform Products). Stamp as desired. Bake as directed; allow to cool. Use rub-ons to color. Mount on page using self-adhesive foam spacers. Mat and mount photos. Print journaling onto transparency; immediately sprinkle with white embossing powder; heat to set. Repeat for photo caption. Adhere over pictures. Stitch hemp cord around journaling block; mount. Cut out fishhook; tie to bamboo border; mount. Print caption onto photo; circle punch and adhere to circle tag (Avery). Mount with self-adhesive foam spacers and hook on fishhook.

Denise Tucker, Versailles, Indiana
Photos: Greg Mathews, Knoxville, Illinois

Fishing

CREATE A SLIDE-OUT JOURNALING FRAME

Frames are no longer just for photos! Mount torn patterned paper (PSX Design) to bottom of background page. Mat and mount photos. Add crumpled copper cardstock to corner. Set eyelet in bottom photo, and two more in bottom right corner of page. String fiber through; secure from behind. Cut frame from remaining crumpled cardstock. Set eyelets in corners; add wire and fiber. Mount torn strips of vellum to back of frame; mount to page, leaving room for title and journaling card. Stamp title (Hero Arts) and print journaling onto cardstock. Attach fishhook to top with strip of cardstock affixed by eyelet; slide behind frame. Mix adhesive (USArtQuest) with pigment powders (Jacquard) and organic materials to make a paste. Spread over torn pieces of cardstock to create "rocks". Attach to bottom of frame. Finish page with fiber-wrapped paper and metal fish (Craft Etc.!).

Valerie Barton, Flowood, Mississippi

Wide Open Spaces
CAPTURE OFF-THE-BEATEN-PATH PHOTOS

Let beautiful photos to tell the whole story. For background pages, mat cloud patterned papers (Club Scrap) to light blue papers. Mat enlarged photo on cardstock and vellum. Adhere to larger double mat. Using letter stamps (All Night Media), stamp location on vellum matted and inked tag. Attach charm (A Charming Place), fibers and eyelet. Attach to fiber strung across bottom of photo. Mat and mount remaining photos. Adhere matted cardstock strips across both pages; attach with brads. Cut title from paper and ink with pigment ink (Chatterbox) to age; adhere to page. Use wheat stamp (JudiKins) on tag; ink edges. Tie off with fibers, mat and mount to left page. Ink edges of paper stamped with aromatherapy stamp (Club Scrap); double mat off center and affix to right page. Print saying and ink edges. Mat to vellum and mount.

Sherri Brady, Victoria, British Columbia, Canada

The road was new to me,
As roads always are when going back.
–Sarah Orne Jewett

During our drive "home" for Thanksgiving, we were treated to this beautiful scenery. The snow-covered mountains, beautiful blue skies with wispy white clouds... the usual ruggedness of our little part of the world was softened by Mother Nature. Yet another thing for which we were thankful.
Southwestern Virginia, 2002

The Road Was New To Me

MELT COLORED GLUE STICKS

Glue sticks are becoming the newest trend in scrapbooking! Print title and journaling onto background page. Enlarge photo to 5 x 7". Create mat from handmade paper. Cut slices off gold-colored glue stick (AMACO) and lay on mat corners. Heat with embossing tool until melted; set mosaic tiles (Sarah Heidt) in melted glue. Mat on gold swirl paper (Metropolis Paper Company); adhere to page. Affix small section of gold swirl paper to lower corner; add scrap of netting and piece of torn handmade paper. Melt glue sticks and add tiles, fiber and charms (Boutique Trims).

Jane Rife, Hendersonville, Tennessee

The End of the Trail

FRAME WITH DISTRESSED PAPERS

Layering distressed paper makes a beautiful frame for a beautiful photo. Begin by enlarging photo. Mount to background page. Distress each layer of cardstock by wetting, crumpling, flattening out, inking and chalking to give it the look of leather. Cut opening for picture and roll back edges. Start small and work your way to larger openings with each layer so that all the layers show. Mount the layers on top of each other for added dimension. Print title and journaling; crumple, tear, chalk, and mount with self-adhesive foam spacers. To complete, add leather lacings (Darice, Tandy Leather Company), feathers (Crafts Etc.!) and tied deer antler buttons (Jean Allen) at bottom and top of page.

Andrea Lyn Vetten-Marley, Aurora, Colorado
Photo: Kelli Noto, Centennial, Colorado

The End of the TRAIL!

It is NOT A ROAD FOR THE SQUEAMISH! Skyline Drive sits a 1,000 feet above the valley floor on a razor ridge that is barely wide enough for the one-way route. The pavement twists and turns atop the rocks and looks like it ends in the middle of the sky. There are no guardrails separating the vehicles from the sharp drop-offs on the sides and the feeling of danger hangs heavily in the air during the three-mile drive. If your stomach stops flipping long enough to look around, the view of Cañon City, Colorado will take the breath away.

Deer Valley

COMBINE SEPIA AND COLOR PHOTOS

Take a fun technique such as layering sepia and colored photos, add a fun recipe, and you have a fantastic layout. Start with a color and a sepia copy of each photo. Cut portions from photos as desired with craft knife and square punch. Match and adhere cut sepia pieces to color photos and color pieces to sepia photos. Mount blue cardstock (Bazzill) to metallic paper (Paper Adventures) for background page. Use self-adhesive foam spacers to mount cut photo piece on focal photo. Mat focal photo on cardstock, then to larger piece of embossed paper (Paper Adventures). Die cut title letters (QuicKutz) and adhere to bottom of mat. Adhere remaining photos to pages. To finish, affix recipe, map book and snowflake buttons (Jesse James). Add square concho (Scrapworks) with sepia photo inside to enlarged photo.

Tina Coombes, Langley, Berkshire, England

If We Could Freeze Time

GIVE A LAYOUT A WINTER FEEL

Use a simple kitchen staple to stamp a unique background. Crumple plastic wrap, dab on white ink pad, and stamp all over background handmade paper and vellum. Tear patterned vellum (EK Success) in mountain pattern; mount to background. Stamp (Wordsworth) title with blue ink. Outline letters with white pen. Adhere metal letters (Scrapyard 329). Stamp clock (Post Modern Design) and outline. Double mat photos; adhere. Print journaling block. Add details with stamps (PSX, Hero Arts) to journaling block; tear top edge. Ink edges of journaling block with white ink. Attach mesh over journaling with snowflake eyelets (Stamp Doctor). Accordion-fold title bar; chalk creases and add letters with stamps (Hero Arts), inking edges. Mount to page with brads. To finish add snowflake stickers (EK Success).

Holle Wiktorek, Reunion, Colorado

Mammoth Mountain

CINCH IT ALL UP

Use a buckle and ribbon to simulate a belt for a fun page addition. Begin with a brown cardstock background. Tear top from striped paper (Chatterbox); roll edges. Stitch straight edge onto background page about 2" up. Tear piece of patterned paper (Chatterbox) half the size of striped paper; stitch straight edge onto striped paper, including top of main photo. Print journaling onto snowflake paper (Paper Adventures); tear bottom edge and stitch straight edge onto top of background page. Add letter stickers (Chatterbox) for title. Cut section from dark brown cardstock for photos; adhere. Slip ribbon through buckle; affix across striped paper and brown cardstock and secure behind page. Mount remaining photos.

Diana Hudson, Bakersfield, California
Photos: Mona Shield Payne, Henderson, Nevada

The layout shows a snowboarding page titled "BOARD" with the journaling text:

ADVENTURES IN SNOWBOARDING

CHARLIE AND CASEY MADE THE BIG SWITCH FROM SKIING TO SNOWBOARDING WHILE WE WERE IN LAKE TAHOE THIS YEAR. I LOVED IT WHILE THEY WERE LEARNING THE ROPES BECAUSE THEY HAD TO GO NICE AND SLOW. IT DIDN'T TAKE LONG, HOWEVER, BEFORE THEY WERE FLYING DOWN EVEN THE DIFFICULT RUNS. OH WELL, I DON'T MIND BEING THE LAST ONE DOWN, REALLY.

Board

ACCENTUATE A WINTRY LAYOUT WITH METAL PAGE ACCENTS

Bold colors and metal accents combine to create a simple yet striking layout. Trim edges of blue cardstock and mat on black cardstock. Computer journal onto white cardstock; cut into large rectangle block and adhere to blue cardstock. Mat photo with black cardstock and mount on journaling block. Cut two 2½" strips of wire mesh (Scrapyard 329) and adhere to top and bottom of page with white brads. Create title by dangling metal letters, snowflake and tag (Making Memories) with cropped photo from wire mesh using jump rings (Westrim Crafts). Complete page by adorning wire mesh with metal-rimmed tags (Avery) stamped with dates; hang from black ball chain (source unknown).

Colleen Adams, Huntington Beach, California

Northern Wisconsin Sledding

PRINT PHOTOS ON ART PAPER

Use a different type of paper to give your photos a canvas look. Spray background page with silver glitter spray (Krylon). Print photos for top and bottom onto fine art matte paper (Printasia by Ilford) and distress edges with craft knife. Mount all photos to page, leaving room at top and bottom for captions. Print all captions onto black cardstock; cut and adhere above or below photos. Using lettering template (Wordsworth), freehand cut title from blue cardstock. Mat to corrugated cardstock and adhere to page. Print and cut remaining title word and adhere to page photo. Craft snowflake embellishments with shrink film (Grafix) and adhere to page.

Heidi Schueller, Waukesha, Wisconsin

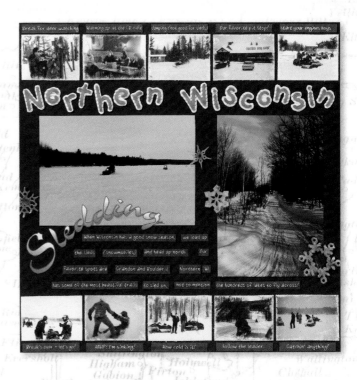

Road Trip To Plum Lake

CRAFT CARDSTOCK AND BEAD ICICLES

Got some chilly photos? Make a chilly layout! Tear paper from a map book that shows where the trip took place. Mount to cardstock. Tear cardstock to form icicle patterns. Apply clear drying glue along edge; add clear beads (Magic Scraps). Allow to dry before mounting to patterned paper (Provo Craft). Mat center photo, leaving room at left for stamped caption. Use letter stamps (Hero Arts) on transparency to create caption; mount on photo mat. Apply glue and beads around edges to form icicles; allow to dry before mounting. Mat fish photo; apply beads to border. Cut part of title from map paper using lettering template (Frances Meyer); mat on cardstock and adhere with self-adhesive foam spacers along with photos. Make fish embellishments using shrink film (Grafix) according to manufacturer directions. Hang embellishment from title with jump rings. Affix rest of title with alphabet pebbles (Making Memories). Finish with paper dolls (EK Success).

Heidi Schueller, Waukesha, Wisconsin

Boot Lake Campground

INCORPORATE A VARIETY OF TEXTURES

Create an earthy feel within you layouts with great textures. Tear strip down right side of sand-patterned paper (Sandylion). Mount to brown background. Cut sections for corner pieces from burlap. Age by chalking, fraying edges, and creating small holes; adhere. Mat and adhere photos. Cut title from textured paper using template (DJ Inkers); stitch around edges and mount with self-adhesive foam spacers. Stamp remaining part of title on torn scrap; chalk, and hang with hemp from brad in corner. Add dragonfly eyelets (Dolphin Enterprises) to photos. Punch circles from brown cardstock for tags; ink and stamp (Hero Arts); adhere to tags and hang from dragonflies with hemp. Print journaling; cut, chalk, and double mat to corrugated cardstock. Adhere to page.

Heidi Schueller, Waukesha, Wisconsin

Adventure

PITCH A FABRIC TENT ON A CAMPING PAGE

Make a fun camping-themed custom fabric frame. Trim and tear patterned paper (Creative Imaginations); mount to background page. Adhere bottom photo to cardstock; tear, chalk edges and mount. Print onto vellum; affix to page with eyelets. Run hemp through bottom; secure to back of page. Cut tent shape from fabric using patterned scissors on bottom. Use craft knife to cut opening in tent; roll flap down and tie with hemp. Adhere to page over photo. String hemp from eyelets to top of tent. Attach twine ends with brads. Apply date at top of page with date stamp (Making Memories); cover with metal frame (Making Memories). Attach large chalked definition stickers (Making Memories) to torn chalked cardstock; adhere to tag. Set eyelet with fabric piece on tag; string with hemp and hang from stick. Finish with additional chalked definition embellishments.

Valerie Barton, Flowood, Mississippi

Badlands

MAKE A LAYOUT ON FOAM BOARD

Give your layout a shadowbox feel with foam board. Cut photo openings from board with craft knife. Adhere handmade paper (Magenta) to board. Working on the back, make slices in the handmade paper through the opening from corner to corner to form an X. Apply adhesive on edges and back of foam board; wrap pieces around back of board to secure. For focal photo, add bronze paper clips (Foofala) to corners before mounting photo on back of board. Mount remaining photos. Adhere slices of cut textured paper (Artistic Scrapper) to frame openings. Use lettering template (C-Thru Ruler) to trace title onto double-sided tape sheet (Magic Scraps); cut. Remove top protective cover; add shimmer sand (Magic Scraps). Remove backing; mat on black cardstock. Adhere to page with black cardstock strips. Journal onto transparency using stamps (PSX Design); mount over mesh (Magenta). Finish with bronze plate and sun charm.

Shannon Taylor, Bristol Tennessee
Photos: Robert Taylor, Bristol, Tennessee

Friends

CREATE A POCKETFUL OF EMBELLISHMENTS

Artfully display embellishments inside a sewn net pocket. First, sew tulle onto background patterned paper (Provo Craft), leaving the top open until embellishments are added. Sew closed. Cut strip from green cardstock; tear off bottom; roll up and chalk edge. Poke holes to insert knotted twine; adhere over top edge of pocket. Punch square photos; adhere just above green cardstock. Cover slide mounts with textured paper; hang printed and matted captions with eye pins (Darice). Mount over photos with self-adhesive foam spacers. Embellish with leaves (Jesse James). Print journaling on patterned paper (Provo Craft); mat on torn cardstock and adhere. Roll small sections of textured paper tightly to form faux sticks for title. Cut and glue into letter shapes. Finish by mounting torn, rolled, chalked and knotted twine corner piece.

Heidi Schueller, Waukesha, Wisconsin

Sea World

San Diego, California

August 2002

Feeding the dolphins proved to be quite a challenge for us. There was a big crowd and it wasn't long before the dolphins' tummies were full. But even though we were the very last group to get a turn and needed help from the trainers, it was worth the wait to see the huge smiles on the kids' faces.

Chapter Three
Eye–Opening Excursions

The need for unabashed, high-flying fun knows no age limit, nor does the quest for knowledge and educational enrichment. Vacations that expand our minds, lift our spirits and honor the child within us remain exceptional destination choices. None but theme parks and educational excursions can offer thrills such as those experienced in soaring down steep roller coaster slopes or seeing exotic animals up close and personal. Wild and magical Disney kingdoms continue to enchant and inspire adults and children alike. Big-splashing sea creatures amaze us with their skills and invite us to learn about them from within their underwater worlds. Museums hold the treasures of human progress and innovation, and historical sights and memorials beckon us to remember, reflect and appreciate. When laughter, learning, awe and inspiration are components of your vacation, horizons become more for broadening and less for scenery.

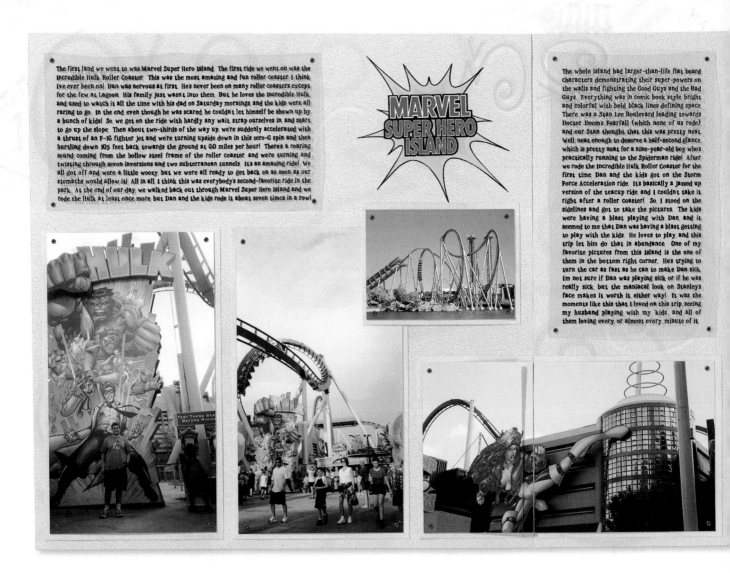

Marvel Super Hero Island

FASHION TITLES FROM MEMORABILIA

Do you ever come home with memorabilia that you are uncertain how to use? Make it into the perfect page title. Silhouette cut title from theme park map; adhere to left side of patterned cardstock background (Club Scrap). Adhere photos to mats with mini eyelets (Making Memories) on both pages, splitting one photo on bottom to bridge the spread. Print journaling onto transparencies and attach to page with eyelets.

Heidi Dillon, Salt Lake City, Utah

Monsters Inc.

CROP PHOTOS INTO FUN SHAPES

Try this nontraditional way of cropping photos for a fun eye-catching effect on graphic patterned paper. Trim photos at random angles; adhere to patterned background pages (SEI). Adhere fibers around photos on left page to frame. Use lettering template (Pebbles Inc.) to cut out title. Print journaling onto vellum and adhere to pages.

Heidi Dillon, Salt Lake City, Utah
Photos: David Dillon, Farmington, Utah

Magic Kingdom
MAKE EMBELLISHMENTS FROM BRADS

Create your own Mickey Mouse embellishments by using various sized brads. Crop, mat and mount photos to patterned background paper (SEI). Print journaling onto vellum; adhere to page with brads (Making Memories). Use two different sizes of brads (Making Memories) to form Mickey Mouse heads and mount along top and bottom of page. Attach title stickers (SEI).

Kim Haynes, Harrah, Oklahoma

Minnie's House
ADD FLARE WITH SERENDIPITY SQUARES

Put your paper scraps to use by making them into embellishments. Begin by printing title and journaling onto dark pink cardstock. Cut a 3¼" wide strip from pink cardstock, leaving length below for Minnie sticker (Sandylion). Adhere strip to light pink background paper. Mount cropped photos to right side of page. Layer small scraps of colored paper on another piece of cardstock. Trim into small squares with paper trimmer and adhere to page, turning slightly to form a diamond. Finish by adding jewels, flower punches and Mickey embellishments (Jesse James) to squares.

Shelby Swartz, Lincoln, Nebraska

Day At Disney
PRINT JOURNALING ON TRANSPARENCIES

Using transparencies is an exceptional way to dress up and add dimension to journaling. Trim patterned background paper (Sandylion); adhere to black cardstock. Assemble and adhere cropped photos on patterned background and apply Mickey sticker (Sandylion). Double mat one photo with cardstock and patterned paper cut in a wave pattern; adhere to right page with star button (Jesse James). Print journaling onto transparency; cut out and adhere over Mickey sticker with button. Print character names in Disney font onto transparency; cut into strips and mount across bottom of page with buttons. For photo envelope, use card holder template (Design Templates Library) and construct from patterned paper. Mount Mickey sticker to patterned paper square with self-adhesive foam spacers and add to bottom left page.

Pam Easley, Bentonia, Mississippi

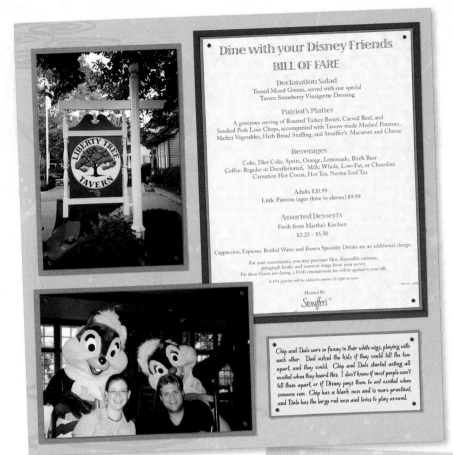

Dine With Your Disney Friends

EMBELLISH WITH VACATION MEMORABILIA

Use a menu from a favorite vacation restaurant for a fun page addition. For left page, double mat menu on red and brown cardstocks; adhere to right side of patterned cardstock background (Club Scrap). Attach photos and journaling to mats with mini eyelets (Making Memories) and add to page. For right page, adhere strip of brown cardstock to right half of background page; mount photos to red photo mats with mini eyelets. Mat journaling on red cardstock with mini eyelets. Silhouette cut embellishment from menu; adhere to top of journaling box.

Heidi Dillon, Salt Lake City, Utah
Photos: David Dillon, Farmington, Utah

Walt Disney World Memorabilia
CREATE EYE-APPEALING SOUVENIR PAGES

Make a page showcasing several of your favorite vacation keepsakes. Use a color-blocking template (Deluxe Designs) to determine placement. Use clear memorabilia pockets (3L Corp.) to hold coin and bill; adhere to page. Mat other souvenirs with cardstock and affix to page; add eyelets to top right mat. Use font from Internet (Lettering Delights) for title. Cut out printed title, mat and adhere to page.

Tiffany McDonough, Long Valley, New Jersey

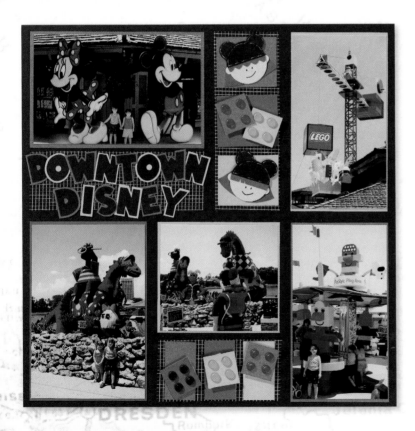

Downtown Disney
PULL ELEMENTS FROM PHOTOS TO CREATE FUN EMBELLISHMENTS

Play up photo elements for a striking page design. Determine placement of photos and embellishments using a color-blocking template (Deluxe Designs). Mat photos and adhere to page. Affix mesh (Magic Mesh) rectangles to page; mount punched letters (EK Success) over one section of mesh for title. Cut or punch squares and rectangles from yellow, red and blue cardstock; adhere to other pieces of mesh. Punch smaller squares from same colors; mount flat-top eyelets (Stamp Doctor) on squares to create "Legos." Mount "Legos" on page with self-adhesive foam spacers. Assemble paper doll heads (EK Success), draw details with black and white pens and adhere to page.

Julia Moncrief, Lakeside, Montana

Jammin' Jungle Drums

RE-CREATE A FAVORITE PHOTO ELEMENT

Paper piecing an element from one of your photos is a great way to accent a layout. Begin by enlarging one photo. Tear strip of sienna cardstock and place it along edge of left page; cut sienna rectangle for journaling block. Mat all photos, leaving extra length at bottom of enlarged photo for decoration. To make patterned strips, use a roller stamp (Stampin' Up!) inked with watermark ink (Tsukineko). Apply color over ink with decorative chalks. Cut out strips, crumple, flatten and adhere to photo mat, journaling block and torn sienna strip. Punch small holes along bottom of mat and through center of journaling block, beneath stamped strips, and thread fibers with beads and charms (All The Extras) through holes. Print journaling on tan cardstock; tear bottom edges and mount to journaling block. Freehand cut drum shapes from patterned paper (Karen Foster Design) and distressed paper. Assemble pieces and mount with fiber over ribbon using self-adhesive foam spacers. Cut out title with craft knife. Punch small squares from handmade paper; cut in half to form triangles and assemble on page. Stitch gold thread through page, knotting on top of holes.

Susan Stringfellow, Cypress, Texas

Animal Kingdom

MAKE AN ENVELOPE FRAME

Try this fun framing technique on your next layout. Tear edges of sand-colored paper, apply brown chalk to edges and layer over page background. Tear squares from animal patterned paper; mount at corners of sand-colored paper and through top center of page. Apply letter stickers (Me & My Big Ideas) to vellum, tear edges and adhere over animal print squares with brads. Add fern die cut (Sizzix) to lower left corner. For envelope frame, start with a 6 x 6" piece of brown cardstock. Measure a 3½ x 5" opening; slice diagonally from one corner of opening to the other, forming four triangle flaps. Tear edges of flaps and chalk. Use cancellation stamp (All Night Media) above top flap. Write "Handle With Care" in brown pen. Turn over, place photo facedown over opening; wrap cardstock edges over and secure with tape. Flip back over; tie with hemp cord. Press flaps back. Journal on tag (DMD) and tie with raffia.

Tracy Burtt, The Woodlands, Texas

Animal Kingdom Lodge is new since we were at Disney last year, so we were anxious to get over there to look around. As soon as we stepped onto the grounds of this resort, it was evident that this is an African themed resort. The lobby has a thatched roof, a mud fireplace and a flowing stream inside. There are hand-carved furnishings, rich wood and vibrant colors. Although it isn't our favorite style, it was beautiful.

The guestrooms of the hotel have balconies that overlook the savannah to see many species of mammals and birds, including giraffe, zebra, gazelle, ostrich, and flamingo. We were able to see the animals from the Savannah overlooks in the public areas.

We had dinner at Boma, the buffet restaurant inside the Lodge. It was truly an African dining experience. Almost all of the employees are Africans, dressed in African clothing. The host greeted us at the door, and gave Michael and Lauren tags with their African names on them, along with the English meaning of the name. Michael's name means Trust, and Lauren's is Charity. They wore these tags throughout our meal. There were many dishes to choose from at the buffet table, none of which we recognized. The chefs behind the tables were very helpful and explained the ingredients in each dish. Most of the food was very spicy and unfamiliar to us. Some of it was very good, but a plateful of spicy food left us with tingling tongues! We enjoyed our dinner, the whole African experience, had a wonderful time together.

African Names
DESIGN DESTINATION-THEMED PAGE ELEMENTS

Re-create the decor of a place you stayed on vacation. Begin by tearing vertical pieces from striped paper (Amscan) for right and left pages. Mount to brown background. Mount photos on torn pieces. Mat cropped photo, leaving room at bottom for raffia. Cut slices in black photo mat and weave raffia through; adhere to page. To make fences, moisten raffia, flatten, cut into short lengths and arrange on cardstock. Mount title on one fence and string of beads on wire on another. Cut small strip of black cardstock and mat on torn tan cardstock; adhere to page with beads strung on wire. For left page, print journaling onto sandy cardstock, tear edges, mat and adhere. Hang tags from beaded floss.

Sue Schneider, Farmington, Connecticut

Epcot

UTILIZE PAGE-LAYOUT TEMPLATES

Short on time? Try page-layout templates to get layouts done quickly. Use color-blocking template (Deluxe Designs) to place photos, title and journaling; crop and adhere accordingly. Cut title letters from cardstock with craft knife; mat and adhere to left page. Print journaling on transparency; adhere transparency over photo covered in vellum.

Heidi Dillon, Salt Lake City, Utah
Photos: Daniel Steenblik, Salt Lake City, Utah

World Showcase – Japan 1995

SHOWCASE A POINT OF INTEREST

One great way to decorate a background is to re-create a point of interest from your photo. Trim gray cardstock and mat on black background. Tear tan cardstock and adhere to bottom of page. Freehand cut archway from cardstock and assemble on page. Crop, mat and mount photos to center of page. Stamp Asian characters (Chronicle Stamps) on cardstock; sprinkle with clear embossing powder and heat to set. Cut out letter, mount on mulberry, tear edges and adhere. For bamboo, freehand cut stalk from green cardstock. Cut pointed strips from lighter green; tie around stalk, press down knot and adhere. Use tied strips on page for embellishment. Write title and journaling with black pens.

Donna Pittard, Kingwood, Texas

Asia

ADD INTEREST WITH PATTERNED PAPER

Use a crackle-patterned stamp to complement a hand-cracked title. Begin by inking edges of background cardstock (Club Scrap). Cut two strips from blue cardstock; stamp with gold ink and crackle-patterned stamp (Stampers Anonymous); ink edges; adhere to pages. Tear sections for both pages from patterned paper (Club Scrap); ink edges and adhere. Print journaling on vellum; apply black embossing powder and heat emboss. Mat journaling and photos to gold metallic paper (Club Scrap); adhere all. For title, cut rectangle from metallic paper; add strip of blue cardstock, beads and cropped photos. Apply letter stickers (Club Scrap) to patterned paper strip; ink and sprinkle with extra thick embossing enamel; heat to set. Bend slightly to make cracks; mount to gold paper.

Heidi Dillon, Salt Lake City, Utah
Photos: Daniel Steenblik, Salt Lake City, Utah

Maui Ocean Center

TRACE A TITLE FROM MEMORABILIA

Emboss over your title to give it a wet look. Begin by cropping and adhering photos onto patterned background paper (Provo Craft). For left page, trace title onto vellum from brochure; ink generously and cover with extra thick embossing powder; heat to set. Repeat process for caption. Double mat title; attach to page with eyelets. Mat caption; mount on envelope (Impress Rubber Stamps) with eyelets and mat again on cardstock. Slip receipts/memorabilia inside envelope. For right page, print journaling on vellum and adhere to center.

Heidi Dillon, Salt Lake City, Utah
Photos: Daniel Steenblik, Salt Lake City, Utah

Kelp forest. Fish. Sharks. Water. Glass.
Divers. Jellies. Sea Turtles. Penguins. Shrimp.
Eels. Tuna. Cameras. Sunfish. Hammerheads.
Octopus. Squid eggs. Starfish. Urchins. Bass
Anenomies. Crabs. 'manda rays'. Divers.
seabirds. Anchovies. Megan. Colton. Garrett.
Jackson. April. Me. Summer vacation.

Monterey Bay Aquarium

INCLUDE PAINTED ACCENTS

Drag a brush with paint over paper to make an artful accent for your pages. Begin by cutting strips from water patterned paper (Paper Adventures); mount vertically to ends of each page. Layer white cardstock over right page; assemble and adhere photos. For left page, enlarge photos to 8 x 10"; crop one down as desired. Mat both and mount to page, layering photos. Print title on white cardstock; cut out and adhere over photo. For painted accents, drag brush with black acrylic paint over white cardstock; let dry. Punch out two medium and three small squares. Mount squares on pages. To complete, print journaling on white; cut out and adhere over white cardstock.

Mary Ann Wise, The Woodlands, Texas
Photos: Colton Wise, The Woodlands, Texas

A Visit To Seal World

MAKE USE OF PHOTO SCRAPS

Use up your extra photos by turning them into embellishments. Trim water patterned paper (Amscan); mat on blue background. Use a color-blocking template (Deluxe Designs) to determine placement of photos, embellishments and journaling. Crop, mat and adhere photos to page. Print journaling inside box onto vellum; cut out and mount with brads. Cut section from underwater photo to fit inside rectangle tag (Making Memories); apply date with stickers and adhere tag. For splashes, freehand cut pieces from water photos; punch photos with a circle punch to make bubbles. Glue beads around bubbles and splashes. String letter beads on wire for part of title; affix to page. Mount second part of title with letter stickers (Creative Imaginations). To finish, adhere dolphin and whale stickers (EK Success).

Pamela James, Ventura, California

YO Ranch

AGE PAPERS FOR ADDED EFFECT

An aged dictionary excerpt adds artistic flare to this layout. Photocopy applicable section from dictionary (Merriam Webster); tear and age with chalk and sepia ink. Highlight definition of interest with yellow vellum; adhere to green cardstock background of left page. Mount photos. Punch letters (QuickKutz) for title from aged cardstock that has been aged with chalk and sepia ink; adhere. For right page, mat top photos to strip of aged cardstock; affix to page. Print journaling onto vellum; tear out, chalk edges and adhere over aged cardstock. Tie fiber around bottom of journaling box and left page; secure to back. Mount remaining photos on right page along with journaling box to complete.

Pam Sivage, Georgetown, Texas

1983. We took a jeep tour of the YO Ranch in Kerrville. We loaded into an open jeep and toured the ranch, looking at all the animals. There was an ostrich that had laid eggs and she was very possessive about her nest. The guide got out of the jeep to open the gate, which was too close to the eggs and the ostrich chased and tried to kick the guide. It was funny, but then we were safe in the jeep. We went inside the ranch house and took a tour of all the trophy mounted animal heads.

This chocolate colored black bear was one of several bears we had the opportunity of watching for a couple of hours. He rummaged through the spring grasses, eating his fill of the tender new growth. We also watched a mother black bear with her young four-month-old cub. Unfortunately, we didn't spot them until later in the evening, and it was much too dark for good pictures.

We were lucky enough to have a ranger stop by and she taught us many facts we didn't know about these magnificent bears. They mate in June or July. They have their babies while they are in hibernation sometime around January. They don't sleep straight through during hibernation. They often wake up, take care of the young, mull around, then return to sleep. They emerge from their dens in late April or early May after the cubs are about three months old. The cubs only weigh about one pound when they are born and are totally helpless. When they first come out of their dens, the cubs are around six pounds. They are amazing climbers. We watched a small bear cub climb about 25 feet high in a matter of a few seconds.

These bears are pretty acclimated to having humans watching them, but we were still very sure to give them plenty of space. What an awesome thing to be able to see these amazing creatures in their natural habitat. Haley's excitement was very contagious and the fact that all three of us were experiencing this for the first time in our lives made it even more special.

BEARS

JUN 3 2003

Bears

MAKE A SINGLE PHOTO THE CENTRAL FOCUS

Build a striking layout by focusing on one exceptional photo. For background, cut two sections from patterned paper (Hot Off The Press); mount on brown cardstock. Print journaling onto striped paper (Hot Off The Press); cut out and adhere to narrow section on background. Cut four triangles and two thin strips from patterned paper. Mount triangles to corners of page and strips to larger section of patterned paper. Mat enlarged photo; adhere to page. Brush lacquer (Ranger) over title letters (Hot Off The Press); adhere to page with self-adhesive foam spacers.

Jodi Amidei, Memory Makers Books

Exotic Animal Paradise

SPOTLIGHT SPECIAL PHOTOS
WITH CIRCLE CROPPING

Small, circle-cropped photos provide a way to showcase many pictures in a unique design. Cut thin strip from patterned paper (C-Thru Ruler); mount across top of brown background cardstock. Stamp date with letter and number stamps (Stampers Anonymous) at top right of page. Use circle cutter (Creative Memories) to crop photos and create mats; adhere photos to page. Write title letters on patterned paper (Colorbök); cut out and double mat. Lightly chalk letters. Adhere matted title, layering each letter. Add rub-on letters (Woodland Scenics) over letter mats. Cut the rest of title with template and chalk letters. Print journaling on cardstock, cut out, chalk, triple mat and adhere to page.

Leah Blanco Williams, Kansas City, Missouri

Adventures In Aviation

SILHOUETTE IMPORTANT PHOTOS

Give certain photos greater emphasis by silhouetting them. Print title onto patterned paper (Daisy D's); mount to patterned background (Karen Foster Design). Cut strip from airplane-patterned paper (Rusty Pickle); adhere onto bottom of page. Print journaling on vellum, leaving room for photo and tag. Silhouette cut airplanes and mount to page, using self-adhesive foam spacers for one. Crop and mount remaining photos. Print captions onto silver paper; trim to fit inside metal-rimmed tags (Making Memories). Color with metallic rub-ons (Craf-T). Wrap wire around tags and secure on back of page.

Pamela James, Ventura, California

Dinosaur Bones

ADD MICA TILES TO AN EARTHY LAYOUT

Embossing mica can add a unique effect to a layout. Trim patterned paper (Scrap Ease); mat to cardstock background. Adhere coastal netting (Magic Scraps) to left side of page with brads. Add various rivets, brads, sea glass (Magic Scraps), mica tiles, (USArtQuest) and fibers on top of netting (Magic Scraps). Apply stamping ink and metallic embossing powders to mica and heat. Add embossed mica to page. Mat photos and adhere to page along with tickets. For metal label holder, ink edges with black ink, stamp letters (PSX Design) onto sandpaper, cut sandpaper to fit inside label holder and adhere to page with brads. Print journaling onto tan cardstock, leaving space in center for title; cut out. Distress by crumpling and applying walnut ink (7 Gypsies). Ink around edges in black. Print title onto tan cardstock; cut out and distress in same way. Adhere over fibers onto journaling block. To complete, add spiral paper clips, pebbles and skeleton leaves to page.

Trudy Sigurdson, Victoria, British Columbia, Canada

Smithsonian

CRAFT A PHOTO TAG

Showcase a special photo by matting it on a tag. Begin by printing journaling onto patterned paper (Club Scrap); cut paper into a half circle and mount to background (Club Scrap). Print title vertically onto cardstock; tear into strip, chalk edges and mount to page. For photo tag, mat photo on cardstock; tear and chalk edges and mount on tag. Tie fibers through tag and adhere to page. Crop, mat and adhere remaining photos. Use tile letter stickers (Making Memories) and chalked letter stickers (EK Success) to make words.

Pamela James, Ventura, California

Pearl Harbor

MAKE A BOLD STATEMENT WITH METAL LETTERS

Here a metal letter title is complemented by a square brad-adorned journaling block. Begin by trimming tan cardstock; mat to dark brown cardstock background. Cut a vertical strip from light gray cardstock; crumple, flatten and attach beads strung with fibers. Enlarge one photo; crop, mat and adhere to page. Print poem on vellum; cut out and mount over crumpled strip with silver square brads (Making Memories). Adhere remaining matted photo. Apply title by gluing on square metal letters (Making Memories).

Trudy Sigurdson, Victoria, British Columbia, Canada
Photos: Libby Sonley, Victoria, British Columbia, Canada

Gardner Museum

PUT POSTCARDS TO USE ON PAGES

If you've ever wondered what to do with picture postcards, consider using them in place of photos for a unique vacation layout. Begin by cropping and matting desired photos and postcards; mount all to background pages. To hang postcard on left page, poke wire through top corners of mat, twisting off at ends. "Hang" wire around brad. To create pull-out postcard, attach a piece of cardstock to top and bottom of postcard and embellish top with sticker (Mrs. Grossman's). Cut slit in background behind another postcard, slightly narrower than cardstock pieces. Slide postcard through slit—the top edge should catch on the slit, preventing it from sliding all the way in. Write journaling and title onto cardstock; cut out, mat and mount.

Christi Spadoni, Wrentham, Massachusetts

Palace Of Fine Arts

DOWNLOAD EMBELLISHMENTS FROM THE INTERNET

Use images printed from your computer for embellishments on layouts. First, give rose and tan papers a distressed look by crumpling and chalking them. Crop and mat photos, using rose-colored paper as a mat on one photo; adhere photos to brown cardstock background. Add brads to corners of top photo. Cut narrow strip from tan distressed paper; mount to center of page. Apply letter stickers (Creative Imaginations). Set rivets (Chatterbox) into ends of title strip over punched circles of rose paper. Punch squares from distressed paper; mount rivets over circles to bottom of page. Attach thread around rivets. Print caption onto distressed rose paper; adhere. Print tickets from Internet (www.exploratorium.edu/palace) onto cardstock, cut out and adhere to page with brads.

Karen Robinson, Cumberland, Rhode Island

Catacombes

TUCK TRAVEL BROCHURES IN A SEWN POCKET

House memorabilia inside a vellum pocket that's sewn onto your page. Cut vellum rectangle for pocket; sew across top edge with sewing machine. Place vellum over brown cardstock background and sew sides and bottom to page. Slip in memorabilia. Attach tickets to front of vellum pocket with clear photo corners (3L Corp.). Mat photos and postcard and adhere to pages. Print journaling onto vellum, leaving open space at bottom; adhere to left page with brads. Silhouette one photo at bottom of journaling. Apply stickers (Club Scrap) for title.

Heidi Dillon, Salt Lake City, Utah
Photos: Heather Quinton, Sandy, Utah

History

FOCUS ON JOURNALING IN A CLEAN DESIGN

Strong layouts sometimes come in the simplest form. Trim cream cardstock and mat to black cardstock background. Mat photo on black; print journaling on white, mat with black and adhere all to page. Apply rock sticker (Me & My Big Ideas) to journaling. Write date on rock with black pen. Cut title letters from cardstock with a craft knife, using a computer font as a guide.

Dee Gallimore-Perry, Griswold, Connecticut

Mayflower

TEAR A BACKGROUND FOR ADDED TEXTURE

Create an interesting background by pulling colors from your photos and layering torn sections. Tear strip from sand-colored cardstock; mount to center of beige background. Tear larger section of light blue cardstock and adhere, leaving some of background showing at top. Cut title with a craft knife from brown cardstock; affix at top. Print journaling and caption onto sand cardstock, leaving room in journaling for torn strip at center. Cut out caption in a tag shape. Mat tag, journaling and photos; adhere photos. Add torn blue strip and sticker (Karen Foster Design) to journaling. Attach journaling and tag to page with eyelets.

Dee Gallimore-Perry, Griswold, Connecticut

Rocky Ridge Farm

FEATURE HISTORICAL INFORMATION

A quick way to journal about historical facts is to take photographs of information plaques. Print title on cream background page. Cut blue strip and adhere to center of left page. Enlarge and crop photos of information plaques and adhere below blue strip. Mat and adhere remaining photos for right page. Print journaling onto transparencies; cut out and adhere. Download book covers from Internet; print, cut out and mount along bottom of right page.

Amy Alvis, Indianapolis, Indiana

On our way to Branson Missouri, Dad and I stopped in Mansfield. This is the home of Laura Ingalls Wilder, whom is one of my favorite authors. I read all of her books growing up and watched the TV series every week. It was late in the season when we got there (they had closed the weekend before) so we were not able to take a tour of Laura and Almanzo's home. We were able to get into the gift shop and Dad purchased several books to give me at Christmas time.

This is the view from Laura's front porch. I can just imagine her sitting on this porch looking out over her land and writing her books. It was so neat to be standing where Laura had stood and seeing the view that she had seen for so many years. I am so glad that we were able to stop and visit the farm. This is one of my favorite memories and I will treasure it for the rest of my life!

ANNEX STATION

"Mount Rushmore began to emerge from granite in South Dakota's Black Hills in 1927. A vision of Gutzon Borglum born in Idaho in 1867, the son of Danish Mormons, studied art in Paris and worked on the project until he died in March of 1941. His son Lincoln supervised completion and carving came to an end in October 1941."
National Park Service, U.S. Department of the Interior

LaNd

oF tHe

FREE

Comprised of George Washington–commander of the Revolutionary army and first U.S. President. Next is Thomas Jefferson; author of the Declaration of Independence, third President and advocate of westward expansion. Set further back in the mountain is our nations 26th President, Theodore Roosevelt who promoted construction of the Panama Canal and ignited progressive causes such as conservation and business reform. Finally on the far right is Abraham Lincoln–Americas 16th President whose leadership restored the Union and ended slavery on U.S. soil.

Chapter Four
America the Beautiful

From sea to shining sea, America is home to an astonishing array of vacation-worthy wonders. From Lady Liberty's gilded torch to San Francisco's Golden Gate, America invites all those in search of new horizons to experience the beautiful and bountiful United States. You may choose to explore the sleek city skyscape of New York, the bewitching historical background of Salem, the patriotic appeal of Washington D.C., or the smooth southern charms of Charleston. Maybe you'll wish to take in the sheer wonder of the sweeping St. Louis Arch, a Texas-sized helping of southern hospitality in Dallas, or the rustic and rugged beauty of Albuquerque. Maybe it will be the majestic Rocky Mountains of Colorado, unspoiled open spaces of the Dakotas, or wild frontier of Wyoming that will dictate your choice of destinations. Like many starry-eyed sight-seers, perhaps you'll continue westward and experience the glamour of Hollywood or head up the coast to peruse the wave-lapped ports and bustling piers of Seattle. Anywhere your compass steers you, in America your travels will be both unparalleled and unforgettable.

Statue Of Liberty

FINISH OFF PHOTO MATS WITH DECORATIVE SCISSORS

Use decorative scissors to give your photo mats some pizazz. Apply photo corners (Canson) to postcard and photos. Create select photo mats by trimming off-white and oatmeal cardstock with decorative scissors (Provo Craft). Single and/or double mat postcards and photos; mount on patterned paper background (Northern Spy). Print journaling onto off-white cardstock; mat on oatmeal cardstock and mount on right and left background pages. Computer print title; cut with craft knife and mount above journaling. Mat Statue of Liberty stamp and circle-punched photo on punched circles; affix to page.

Heidi Dillon, Salt Lake City Utah
Photos: Daniel Steenblik, Salt Lake City, Utah

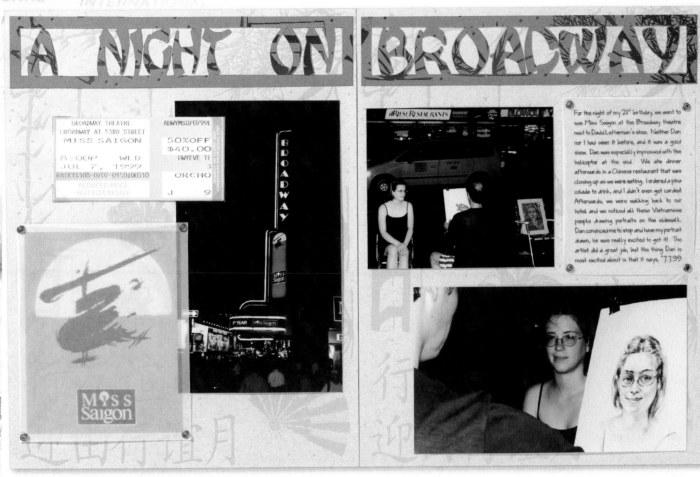

A Night On Broadway

SILHOUETTE CUT A TITLE

Use a craft knife to create a spectacular title for your vacation layouts. Mount photos and postcard to patterned paper (Club Scrap). Print journaling on vellum; cut to size and mount to background with eyelets. Mount vellum block over mounted postcard with eyelets. Mount theater ticket using clear photo corners (3L Corp.). Create title using Oriental font and Oriental-themed paper (Club Scrap). Use a computer to print title, placing it inside a frame. Print onto patterned paper. Use a craft knife to cut away negative spaces, leaving letters and frame intact; adhere to page.

Heidi Dillon, Salt Lake City, Utah
Photos: Daniel Steenblik, Salt Lake City, Utah

Our Vacation Started In New York

CREATE A DIGITAL LAYOUT

Create a cutting-edge digital layout of your journey. This page was created in Photoshop 7.0 (Adobe). Create the frame template using the blending option to give them a 3-D effect. Add frame embellishments and text to frames. To "hang" frames, create "ribbons" with translucent rectangles. Use blending options to create 3-D effects. Create buttons by adding bevel and embossing to circles. Finish with panoramic photo and title. To re-create this layout as a traditional scrapbook page, use embellished slide mounts or metal frames for cropped photos. Hang with ribbon and large brad. Mat and mount panoramic photo to bottom of page. Cut title from cardstock or print on title strip; adhere to page.

Laura Vanderbeek, Logan, Utah

New York City And The Brooklyn Bridge

CREATE A DIGITAL LAYOUT

Use your computer to create a layout featuring stamped images. This striking digital layout was created using Photoshop 7.0 (Adobe). Create stamp template by starting with a rectangle and deleting partial circles from edges. Create drop shadow; duplicate and re-size as needed. Background texture was created using the herringbone texture blending option. Add photos and text. To re-create this layout as a traditional scrapbook page, cut stamps with decorative-edged scissors. Mat photos and mount over stamps; adhere to page with foam spacers. Print journaling to cardstock; mat and mount. Adhere title and panoramic photo.

Laura Vanderbeek, Logan, Utah

Freedom Is Not Free

TEAR A FAUX FLAG

Combine star and stripe patterned papers to create a flag with a vintage feel. Tear away a square-shaped window in the top left corner of striped patterned paper (Provo Craft); roll back edges. Mount blue star patterned paper (Provo Craft) behind exposed window. Hand journal onto vellum; cut out journaling block and mount to lower right corner of page. Print "Freedom is not" on vellum and mount in upper left corner. Use letter stickers (Creative Imaginations) on vellum to create remainder of title and mount.

Ari Macias, Staten Island, New York

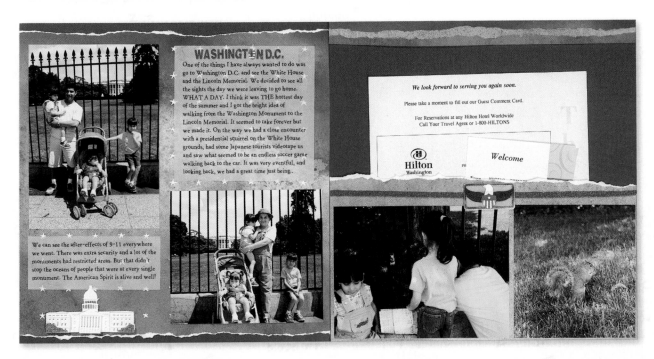

Washington D.C.

USE POCKET PAGES TO STORE MEMORABILIA

Construct pockets for your travel maps and receipts. For left page create background by tearing the top and bottom edges from patterned paper (Provo Craft); adhere to dark blue cardstock. Mount photos. Print journaling on vellum; cut into blocks and mount. Embellish with stickers (EK Success). For right page, tear a section from patterned paper (Provo Craft) approximately half the size of background page to create pocket. Adhere side and bottom edges of pocket paper to background cardstock. Mount photos on pocket. Add fibers across top; secure on back of page. Tear strips of patterned and red paper and adhere to top of background for border. Embellish with metal rimmed tag (Making Memories) decorated with patriotic sticker (EK Success). Fill pocket with memorabilia.

Ari Macias, Staten Island, New York

The Gettysburg Address

CREATE A DIGITAL LAYOUT

This striped and star-spangled layout was created on a computer. Using Photoshop 7.0 (Adobe), create the blue square and star template adding texture through the blending options. Duplicate and re-size as needed. Form striped pattern adding texture through blending options. Create and layer text on stripes. To form stitching effect on photo, create a "dashed line" stroke, adding effects through blending options. Create title with outer-glow blending option. To re-create this layout in a traditional format, use flag patterned paper for background pages. Use star punches or stickers on blue cardstock for square embellishments. Stitch photo onto mat. Mat photos of Gettysburg Address onto cardstock; adhere to right page. Form title and captions with letter stickers.

Laura Vanderbeek, Logan, Utah

A Monumentally Beautiful City

CUT STICKERS FOR DIMENSION

Create a high-impact patriotic spread with bold red, white and blues. Tear star patterned paper (Sweetwater) in half; adhere pieces to top of left and bottom of right pages. For left page, mount upper left photo on white cardstock. Tear and ink lower cardstock edge; embellish with fiber and mount. Mount remaining photos. Cut out red border sticker (Karen Foster Design); affix to bottom of left page. Print journaling on white cardstock; tear and ink lower edge and mount to background with brads. Embellish with cut-out (EK Success). Use letter stamps (Hero Arts) on vellum to create title; tear, add fiber and mount. Embellish with cut-out (EK Success). For right page mount photos. Add red border sticker embellished with cut-outs (EK Success, Pebbles, Inc.). Mount small square punched photos and add additional cut-outs.

Pam Canavan, Clermont, Florida

Historic

USE VELLUM JOURNALING TAGS ATOP PHOTOS

If you find yourself running out of room for journaling, try this great technique. Cut two strips of patterned paper (Creative Imaginations), approximately the width of background paper. Adhere strip vertically to left page and horizontally to right. Add border stickers (Creative Imaginations) to patterned border strips. Crop and mat photos on sienna cardstock blocks, tearing off bottom edges of blocks; adhere to background pages. Use letter stickers (Creative Imaginations) to create title. Journal on punched (EK Success) vellum tags and adhere atop photos with brads.

Ari Macias, Staten Island, New York

A Link To The Past

EMBOSS STICKERS FOR AN EXTRAORDINARY EFFECT

If you have the perfect sticker, but the colors just don't go with your layout, emboss it. Tear edges from patterned paper (Creative Imaginations); double mat to green and black cardstocks. Mat vertical photo and mount with remaining unmatted photos on page. Print title on vellum and tear edges, leaving room at lower edge for sticker. To emboss sticker (Mrs. Grossman's), ink with embossing ink, sprinkle with black embossing powder and heat to set. Peel sticker from protective background and mount to vellum.

Ari Macias, Staten Island, New York

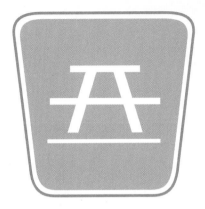

Salem, Massachusetts

CROP PHOTOS FOR A SPECIAL EFFECT

Enlarge and crop photos to create drama as seen on this spread featuring striking historical grave markers. Form background by layering varied sizes of green, yellow and purple cardstock. Enlarge headstone photos; cut out headstones and adhere to bottom of background papers. Double mat additional photos on green and purple cardstock and mount to background. Print title and journaling on cream cardstock; crop to size and mount on page, using brads to secure the title.

Pamela James, Ventura, California

Wisconsin State Capital

CREATE VELLUM PHOTO MATS

Use colored vellum as mats for a subtle yet striking effect. For left page, print journaling onto cream cardstock; trim and mount onto tan cardstock background. For main photo on left page, double mat off-set on green and cream vellum blocks. Mount to background directly above journaling block. Adhere cropped additional photo to lower left portion of page. For right page, double mat photos on green vellum block and cream cardstock; mount on tan cardstock background. Cut small strips from spare photos; affix on either side of small punched vellum square at bottom of page.

Jamie Edge, Sun Prairie, Wisconsin

Wisconsin
State Capital

During Larry and Katie's stay with us, we decided to show them around downtown Madison. After visiting the Monona Terrace we walked down to the State Capital. We decided not to go on the tour, and instead explored things on our own. The murals were absolutely beautiful. The building was decorated for Christmas and the Christmas tree was huge. Nearly every town in Wisconsin was represented on the tree, hanging an ornament in honor of their town. It was very chilly outside, so afterwards we stopped at a coffee shop to warm up.

December 28, 2001

I was completely enthralled & captivated by the details of the architecture. I could have stayed here for hours.

Balboa Park

Balboa Park

PAIR PICTURES WITH PATTERNED PAPER

Make it look as if you spent hours stamping a background with this printed cardstock. Trim select sections from printed cardstock (Club Scrap); adhere sections to right and left cardstock background pages. For left page, crop and mat photo off-set in upper corner. Mount unmatted remaining photo. Stamp flowers (Club Scrap) below matted photo; journal. Write title on tan cardstock block; mat and adhere to left page. To finish, adhere both matted and unmatted photos to right page.

Christi Spadoni, Wrentham, Massachusetts

Historic Charleston
PLAY OFF OF PATTERNED PAPER DESIGNS

Utilizing patterned papers can be tricky. Start by pairing your papers with photos that complement the hues present in the paper design. For left page, cut a 5" wide strip of black cardstock and mount on left side of pinstripe patterned background paper (SEI). Cut a slightly narrower section from teal paper; tear bottom edge and adhere on top of black border strip section. Mount matted photo to strip. Apply title to tag with letter stickers (Provo Craft) and mount on border strip. For right page, start by slicing vertical photo into sections; affix to lower right side of page, leaving narrow spaces between cropped sections. Mat remaining vertical photo. Mount it and unmatted photos to background. Embellish with tag created by stacking varied sizes and colors of cardstock circles; attach to double-matted block and decorate with a button.

Barb Hogan, Cincinnati, Ohio

Barb and Terri walked all over historic Charleston and shopped in the outdoor markets while the others went boating for the day.

Tour Guide

MAKE A LACE-UP POCKET PAGE

Faux pockets are an artistic and useful way to embellish a layout. Tear edges from teal striped patterned papers (Design Originals); chalk edges and mat to black background pages. For left page, mat photo on corrugated paper (DMD); tear off bottom mat edge. Mount on background. Distress printed "Clarksville" paper (computer created); tear off section and mat to a piece of torn black cardstock for title block. Stamp tag messages "Tour" and "Welcome" (PSX Design) on cardstock; trim to size and fit under metal tags (Making Memories). Mount tags on corrugated paper; mount on title block and to bottom of photo. Cut "guide" portion of title using dies (Sizzix) and adhere to title block. Make gate-fold card from cardstock; tear upper edge and chalk. Set eyelets and fold in sides and bottom; lace. Tuck memorabilia inside. For right page, tear corner from distressed printed paper; adhere lower and right edges to background paper. Add memorabilia, adhering it to page. Mount matted photos, printed and matted L-shaped journaling block and embellishments to finish.

Holle Wiktorek, Reunion, Colorado

Sights Of Tucson
PUNCH OUT PHOTO ELEMENTS

Punch tiles from larger photos for a dynamic layout. Triple layer graduated sizes of brown, peach and gold cardstock to form background page. Punch square photo tiles from larger photos; mat and mount on background page. Hand journal on gold paper; double mat and mount. Use conchos (Scrapworks) to create date. Stamp "Sights Of" portion of title on background (All Night Media) and create the remainder of the title with leather string. For dream catcher embellishment, punch center from metal rimmed tag. Wrap with embroidery floss, adding beads as you work; add charm (ScrapArts) and mount on triple-matted block. Cover lizard with adhesive and foil flakes (Anima Designs) before mounting on page.

Shannon Taylor, Bristol, Tennessee

Santa Fe Indian Market
CREATE A CRACKLED LOOK FOR AN EYE-CATCHING TITLE

Embellish with copper rub-ons for a southwestern glow. Mat two photos on black cardstock; mount in upper right and lower left corners of sienna cardstock background; mount remaining large unmatted photo in lower right corner. Cut rectangle from patterned paper (Amscan) for title/journaling block. Print journaling on sienna cardstock; cut and mount on lower half of title/journaling block. Print and cut out "Santa Fe" title letters. Cover with 4-5 layers of extra thick embossing powder; heat set, cool and bend to crack. Mount over freehand cut teal cardstock zigzag accent. Write subtitle on double-matted strip and mount below title with brads. Use decoupage glue to cover slide mounts with patterned paper (Amscan); adhere cropped photos to backside of slide mounts. Mount lower right slide mount overlapping teal zigzag strip and photo. Mount other slide mounts and embellish with additional teal zigzag strips. Cut suns from copper paper; rub with metallic rub-ons (Craf-T); adhere to page, tucking behind slide mounts and photos. Add sun buttons (JHB International).

Michelle Pesce, Arvada, Colorado

The Mustangs Of Las Colinas

EMBOSS PHOTO MATS

Add pizazz to your photo mats with embossing enamel. Tear vertical strips from green and orange cardstocks and patterned paper (Club Scrap). Ink edges lightly; cover with extra thick embossing powder; heat set. Layer torn and embossed strips and mount on right side of pumpkin cardstock background. Add brads at corners. Mount smaller matted photos to torn strip border with foam spacers. Double mat large photo on white and green cardstocks. Apply copper ink to mat edges; sprinkle with clear extra thick embossing powder; heat set. Adhere matted photo to page with foam spacers. Create "Mustang" title by stamping on transparency (Wordsworth); emboss using pumpkin-colored embossing powder; mount with brads to right side of main photo. Create journaling block in similar fashion and mount to page.

Jodi Amidei, Memory Makers Books
Photos; Torrey Miller, Thornton, Colorado

Las Vegas – Bright Lights

TEAR AND LAYER PHOTOS

Stack photos for vertical impact. Start by tearing tops and bottoms from photos; adhere to hand-made glittered background paper, layering pictures to form a column. Add gold ribbon to left side of photos with brads. Adhere another piece of ribbon to right side of page; add circle-punched photos mounted to tags (Making Memories). Affix lattice-style ribbon to left side of page. Mount torn photo on top of ribbon. Embellish with hand-journaled words set in gold frames (Nunn Design).

Polly McMillan, Bullhead City, Arizona

The Arch– St. Louis

MAKE ARTFUL USE OF METALLIC PAPER

Try matting title and journaling blocks on metallic paper for a little flair. Begin by mounting all photos to blue sparkled paper (Paper Garden). Adhere mounted photos to blue background cardstock on both pages. Print journaling on vellum block; cut to fit over vertical photo on right page. String fiber along bottom of journaling block; securing to page with silver brads. To finish right page, add pewter sticker (Magenta), fibers and brad embellishment. For left page, cut arched piece from silver paper; adhere to background on lower right corner. Stamp letters (Stampendous) on sparkled blue cardstock blocks; sprinkle with silver embossing powder and heat to set. Mat stamped blocks to silver paper. Adhere title to page with fiber and brads; adhere date box. Embellish with pewter sticker (Magenta).

Valerie Barton, Flowood, Mississippi

Meet Me In St. Louis

CREATE A PHOTO-INSPIRED BACKGROUND ELEMENT

Mimic the focal point in your photos with a graceful arched embellishment. Freehand draw arch on cream cardstock; cut and adhere to blue cardstock background. Trim ½" from left edge of blue cardstock background; mount 1" red strip on left side of blue cardstock background to form border. Cut sheet of patterned vellum (Chatterbox) slightly narrower than blue cardstock background. Cover arch with patterned vellum. Adhere border strips cut from brown paper to lower edges of both background pages; adhere rectangular embellishment boxes created from patterned paper (Chatterbox) to border strips with eyelets. Affix die-cut title letters (QuickKutz). Freehand draw branch on cardstock; cut out, chalk and mount to top of left page. Cut leaves using a die cut (Sizzix); chalk and adhere to "branches". Double mat and mount photos to pages. Print journaling onto vellum; mat and adhere to page with eyelets.

Beverly Sizemore, Sulligent, Alabama

The Golden Gate Bridge

CREATE AN ARTFUL LOOK WITH BLACK-AND-WHITE PHOTOS

Black-and-white photos and coordinating papers combine for a clean and creative layout. For left page, cut photo into vertical sections; adhere to background in top right corner, leaving space between photo pieces. Mat remaining photos and vellum-journaled tag on black cardstock. Cut ½" from right side of larger photo. Adhere cut section with a brad to left side of left-hand page for visual interest. Mount remaining photos to background. For right page, mat vertical photo on black cardstock. Double mat photo of bridge dedication plaque on cream and black cardstock; mount on background patterned paper (SEI). Mount unmatted photo in top left corner. Print journaling onto tag (SEI); mat and adhere with silver brad. Print title onto vellum; tear out and adhere with brads.

Barb Hogan, Cincinnati, Ohio

Exploring Seattle, WA

USE ADVERTISEMENTS AS DESIGN INSPIRATION

Make your layout look like an article by printing journaling in magazine-like columns and employing graphic design style. Use computer software to design title and journaling layout; print onto blue cardstock. Cut out journaling block and adhere to brown cardstock backgrounds. Print date onto green cardstock; cut into narrow strips and adhere across top of journaling block on both pages. Punch photos with 2" square punch and mount side by side along top and bottom of both pages to form horizontal borders.

Joanna Bolick, Black Mountain, North Carolina

Pebble Beach

INCORPORATE A MINI PHOTO ALBUM

Include more photos on your layout with an attached photo album. Create mini album by enclosing photo pockets in corrugated cover. Embellish with patterned papers (source unknown), photo corners, metal accents (Making Memories), letter stickers (EK Success) and photo tag adorned with ribbon. Attach to handmade background paper (source unknown). Make memorabilia envelope from folded handmade paper. Wrap with mesh strips; mount metal frame (Making Memories) and embellished tag (Avery) and adhere to page. Fill with memorabilia. Tear edges from panoramic photo; wrap mesh around ends, add embellished tag and adhere with brads. Tear main photo, double mat and affix over torn panoramic. Add cardstock photo corners. Create title with stickers (K & Co. and Colorbök) and plastic letters (Colorbök) adhered to circle tags adorned with ribbon.

Polly McMillan, Bullhead City, Arizona

Excursion

PAINT TILES FOR ADDED GLOW

Give a Mediterranean feel to your layout with glowing tiles and chalked paper. Create background by lightly rubbing turquoise cardstock with white ink pad. Rub turquoise chalk (Craf-T) on tile paper (Paper Adventures); set with matte fixative. Cut a 1" and a 4" strip of chalked tile paper; mount narrower strip on left side of and wider on right. Print journaling onto transparency; cut and mount to bottom of page. Adhere photos. Prime silver tiles (Scrapyard 329); rub with select shades of acrylic paint (Delta, Plaid). When dry, sand lightly and mount to page. Use rub-on word (Making Memories) across top of photo and page to create title.

Diana Hudson, Bakersfield, California

San Diego

SCRAP A GETAWAY

Use printed metal embellishment tags and metallic silver paper mats for a glitzy touch. Cut horizontal strip from striped patterned paper (source unknown); mat on silver paper strip and adhere across top of red cardstock background page. Adhere a strip of distressed silver paper along the lower edge of patterned paper strip. Mat photos on silver cardstock; mount top left photo at angle so left corner extends beyond background edge. Print title "San Diego" letters onto silver paper; pen black borders, cut out letters and mount on page. Print journaling block on silver paper; cut and double mat on striped patterned paper and silver paper. Attach to background with brads. Add metal word accents (Die Cuts With A View) affixed with eyelets and brads. Complete with "Gaslamp" typewriter key letters (Hot Off The Press).

Pamela James, Ventura, California

Star Gazing

DECORATE PHOTO EDGES WITH GLITTER

Add a sprinkle of glitter to star-shaped photo edges for additional impact. Trim black cardstock and mat on red textured paper (DMD) to form background. Cut stars from photos of Hollywood's famous sidewalk and line edges with gold glitter glue (Duncan). Punch small holes in select stars and hang with gold thread; secure thread to back of page. Die cut title letters (Sizzix) from gold paper. Cut second set of "Star" letters from black cardstock; mat black letters on gold die-cut letters; mount title on background. Hang smaller stars from title. For bottom left photo, outline star with glitter glue; mount to page. Print journaling on cream cardstock; double mat on black and brown cardstocks; mount. Embellish with movie-themed stickers and miniature Hollywood sign (EK Success).

Janetta Abucejo Wieneke, Memory Makers Books

ANNEX STATION

taj mahal

Taj Mahal—a love story. This monument is described as the most extravagant ever built for love. It was constructed by Emperor Shah Jahan in memory of his second wife, Muntaz Mahal, whose death in childbirth in 1631 left the emperor so heartbroken that his hair is said to have turned grey overnight.

After disembarking our camel-drawn cart, we were immediately accosted by a local who offered (for a small fee) to gladly photograph our visit to the Taj Mahal.

Chapter Five
International Intrigue

Fortunate is the holder of an abundantly stamped passport. Within this little book's inked pages is evidence of one's ventures into new frontiers and realms of experience. In traveling beyond our borders, we season our spirits with culture and diversity and return home with newfound appreciation for the world in which we live. With so many unique destinations, from the Americas to the west, Asia to the east, India, the Arctic circle and all else that lie in-between, our itineraries will never be complete as long as we hear the call of adventure. In the English countryside we may listen for the echoes of Shakespearean sonnets, and in Paris, the bustle of quaint coffeehouses on cobblestone streets. In Austria and Switzerland we can watch green hillsides roll gradually into winter-white peaked mountains, and in Italy, water ferries weaving through winding canals. In Egypt we can retrace the footsteps of ancient royalty, and in Africa and Australia explore vast and unspoiled horizons. Our seven continents are truly the seven wonders of the world, each providing limitless opportunities for enriching travel experiences.

First Stamp In Your Passport

RECORD A MILESTONE

There is nothing like scrapbooking a baby's "first," and the first stamp in a passport is extra special. Begin by trimming background paper (Club Scrap) to mat onto black cardstock. Scan, enlarge and print photo from passport; adhere. Scan and enlarge passport cover and one page with stamp for inside of cover; mount both on page. Sand blank credit card (Club Scrap) and stamp title (PSX Design) on it; tie with fibers and adhere. Add fibers to lower page edge with bookplate (Making Memories) mounted over smaller photocopy of passport stamp. Finish with small charm (All The Extras) at top of tag and large metal accent (Making Memories) at bottom.

Sam Cousins, Shelton, Connecticut

The Itinerary Of A Retired Passport

JOURNAL THE STOPS IN YOUR PASSPORT

This is a great way to sum up many trips in one scrapbook spread. Tear half circle from tan cardstock; spray with glitter spray (Duncan) and adhere to left side of patterned paper (Design Originals). Set three pairs of eyelets on circle edge; string fibers through and secure to back of page. Apply title with letter stickers (C-Thru Ruler) and handwriting on small cardstocks strips. Underline with metallic dimensional paint (Duncan). Crop or punch photos into 2½" squares; mount evenly spaced on page. Print corresponding journaling on cardstock squares. Tear vellum wrap-around envelopes; adhere below photos. Add buttons to flaps; slip in journaling. Stamp (Plaid) location of photos onto torn cardstock; chalk and adhere to corresponding envelope. Adhere retired passport directly on page.

Oksanna Pope, Los Gatos, California

The Tower Of London

FEATURE FUNCTIONAL POCKETS

If you have a lot of memorabilia and want to incorporate it all, use pockets on your pages. To form background for right page and some of left, cut brick shapes from distressed paper; outline and adhere to black cardstock. On left page, mount a flat paper bag from vacation gift shop directly on page so that bag may be used to hold memorabilia. Print journaling onto vellum and adhere with mini eyelets. Mat and mount photos; add fabric-matted metal numbers (Making Memories) to upper corners. For right page, attach lower matted photo with self-adhesive foam spacers along bottom and sides; tuck ticket stubs or memorabilia into pocket formed by matted photo. Adhere second matted photo ticket; add fabric and metal accents to both photos. Cut section from page protector large enough to hold pamphlet; affix with square brad fasteners (Making Memories) and place pamphlet inside to finish.

Trudy Sigurdson, Victoria, British Columbia, Canada

Stonehenge

DISTRESS PAPER FOR AN AGED EFFECT

Showcase a stunning vacation photo by enlarging it. Start page by adhering mesh across upper and lower edges of cardstock backgrounds. To distress tan cardstock (Bazzill), spray with water from a squirt bottle; crumple, flatten and let dry. Rub distressed paper with black chalk. Cut letters for title, wrap with hemp twine and adhere. Mount distressed cardstock to both pages, making it flush to center. Use brown pen to line paper around all but center edges. Mat main photo; adhere to both pages by slicing section off, lining up and mounting flush to center on right page of spread. Mat remaining photos; tie hemp twine around bottoms, add beads and affix to right page. Print journaling on cardstock; chalk and draw line around edge. Mat and adhere. Finish with small square punched photos, matted and mounted in corners.

Trudy Sigurdson, Victoria, British Columbia, Canada

England!

ADD DIMENSION TO A GRAPHIC DESIGN

Use self-adhesive foam spacers to add depth to certain areas of your layout for a 3-D effect. Crop desired photos into evenly sized squares and rectangles to form a grid with even spacing between photos. Arrange photos loosely for visual appeal, leaving space for title to be added. For title, cut letters (Sizzix) from blue cardstock; mat with white cardstock. Mount letters with title blocks (Die Cuts With A View) on page using self-adhesive foam spacers for depth. Permanently mount photos, using self-adhesive foam spacers on random photos for depth. Print journaling and date onto transparency film; trim to size and adhere over photos.

Kelli Noto, Centennial, Colorado

Le Chateau

JOURNAL ONTO TRANSPARENCIES FOR TAGS

Sometimes vacation photos capture a great deal of history. An eye-pleasing way to tell the story is with tags. Mat patterned papers (Scrap Ease) to black background pages with eyelets. Mat photos and adhere to pages. Freehand cut tags from green cardstock. Use a stiff stippling brush and green and brown inkpads to dot colored texture onto tags; outline by rubbing inkpad edge along tag edges. Set eyelets in tags and add fibers; mount with self-adhesive foam spacers beneath tags along lower edge of page. Print journaling for each photo onto transparency film; trim to fit tags and adhere. Finish by cutting and mounting letters (QuicKutz) for title.

Heidi Dillon, Salt Lake City, Utah
Photos: Heather Quinton, Sandy, Utah

Paris In A Day

CREATE A PULL-OUT DIARY

To show where you have been on your vacation, create a clever time line that links photos to points on a map and include a hidden diary. Cut a souvenir map to page size and mount on background paper. Tear around outer edges of vellum; lay vellum over map. Use a small shape template, pencil and then a craft knife to trace areas to cut out, exposing only the map areas actually visited. Adhere vellum in place atop map. Cover slide mounts (Quick Point) with handmade paper; add fibers. Use a tag template to trace or a tag punch to punch tag shapes from clear shrink plastic (K & B Innovations). Rub tags with green and brown ink pads to color and write times with black journaling pen. Pierce top of tags with a sewing needle for a hole; heat according to package directions. When cooled, connect tags to slide mounts with jump rings. Cut clear transparency film or a page protector for slide "window" and affix on back; mount over cropped photos on page with self-adhesive foam spacers. Triple the thickness of self-adhesive foam spacers on mount to hold diary. Adhere brad fasteners to page; attach fiber hung from mounts. Cut title letters from shrink, colorize, bake or heat and adhere. For diary, journal onto small pieces of cardstock. Lay a tag on top and bottom of journaling; staple. Use letter stamps (Hero Arts) to label diary; tie off and slip into slide-mount holder. Use stamps for subtitle; adhere to page with brads.

Heidi Schueller, Waukesha, Wisconsin

Paris, France, 1993

PUT MONEY IN YOUR POCKETS

Use self-adhesive memorabilia keepers on your pages to keep mementos such as foreign coins. Use stamp (Hero Arts) and watermark ink (Tsukineko) to stamp background onto green cardstock. Add photo corners (Canson) and adhere to background pages. Mat desired photos and adhere. Stamp journaling (All Night Media, PSX Design); cut into tag shapes and add eyelets. Add fibers and mount on pages. Cut cardstock squares, adhere plastic envelopes (3L Corp.), insert coins and adhere.

Brandi Ginn, Lafayette, Colorado
Photos: Chris Hillman, Provo, Utah

International Intrigue

Doe Den Tap Toe

CREATE HINGED PHOTO COVERS FROM COASTERS

Use hinged coasters collected from your vacation to conceal photos and journaling. Crop photos slightly smaller than the size and shape of coasters; mat with vellum. Arrange photos on page to determine placement of coasters and photos. Print journaling and adhere with photos to page. Attach hinges (Schlage) to coasters and page with brad fasteners over photos and journaling. Cut title from red paper; emboss with several layers of clear embossing powder (Yvonne Albritton Designs). When cool, bend lightly to crack. Mat letters; adhere to vellum and mount on page with nailheads (Chatterbox). Finish with printed journaling strip attached to vellum at bottom of page.

Heidi Schueller, Waukesha, Wisconsin

Seefeld, Austria

SEW VELLUM COIN POCKETS

Make a permanent pocket for memorabilia. Tear vertical border strip from purple vellum; outline edges with silver leafing pen (Krylon) and adhere to purple background. Make envelopes from translucent vellum; tear flaps and line with silver leafing pen. Cut two tags from page protectors or transparency film for each coin; insert coin and sew shut. Repeat for all coins. Add eyelet and fibers to tags; insert into envelopes and mount on border. Mat photos; adhere to page. Emboss cardstock with silver powder. Use letter template (Wordsworth) to cut title from it, mat to blue cardstock and adhere. Use different font for first part of title; cut out and mount. Journal onto vellum; cut out and adhere to metal tags (Making Memories); add metal flower charms (Making Memories). Punch various-sized daisy flowers from vellum; line edges with silver pen. Mount to page with brads.

Heidi Schueller, Waukesha, Wisconsin

Switzerland

ADD AN AGED LOOK WITH SEPIA PHOTOS

Give an old-world feel to your layouts with sepia-tone photos and distressed papers. Form background page from various pieces of patterned papers (Creative Imaginations); chalk and adhere to brown cardstock (Bazzill). Add walnut ink to torn paper's edges. Print photos in sepia color; crop one to fit metal-rimmed tag (Making Memories). Pop out center of tag; wrap frame in ribbon and adhere with remaining photos to page. For journaling tag, use various cut patterned papers (Creative Imaginations) on green cardstock (Bazzill). Spray lightly with walnut ink. Add stamp embellishments (Creative Imaginations). Print journaling onto vellum; tear out, adhere, and add ribbon to top. To complete, apply title with letter stickers and word poem stones (both Creative Imaginations).

Claudine Van Dyne, Woodstock, Illinois

Italy

CREATE A PHOTO CARD

Use a circle punch to crop photos to mount on metal-rimmed tags (Making Memories). Begin with patterned paper (K & Co.); adhere photo corners (Canson) and mount to background page. Insert vertical panoramic photo into photo corners; print caption onto vellum, tear and adhere with brad fasteners. Affix circle-punched photos to metal tags and adhere on page. Create small envelope to hold folded money; adhere and embellish with coin. Fold a piece of cardstock into a vertical card. Adhere journaling and remaining photo inside. For cover, add photo corners to photo, affix atop card and add metal tag embellished with medium fleur-de-lis punch. Use metal letters and metal frame (both Making Memories) for title; add wax seal (Papyrus) to complete page.

Polly McMillan, Bullhead City, Arizona

Blejski Otok

CREATE A SERENDIPITY SQUARE BORDER

Make an attractive border with some paper scraps and a square punch. Adhere several scrap pieces of paper (Club Scrap) on cardstock, layering and overlapping to create a collage. Stamp images (Club Scrap) randomly across collage in coordinating ink colors. Punch small squares from collage; mat and mount as side borders on background paper (Club Scrap). Use lettering template (Cock-A-Doodle Design) to cut title; mat and mount. Mat and adhere photos to left background page. Sew vellum pocket onto cardstock; slip in postcard and adhere. For right page, mat photos, leaving room on one for additional serendipity squares. Add green photo corners to photo and squares to mat; adhere. Mount remaining photos. Print journaling onto vellum; adhere to page with eyelets.

Heidi Dillon, Salt Lake City, Utah
Photos: Heather Quinton, Sandy, Utah

September 9, 2001 – We walked down to the lake taking the shortcut that Mary Beth and I had discovered the night before. We ate a simple lunch at a little cafe that overlooked the water. After lunch, we walked down to the docks and talked to the pletna drivers about getting us over to the island. It was a little chilly, and Betty was worried about going to the island in a boat, she asked how deep the water was and if there were life jackets. Since she was so nervous about going in an open pletna, our driver took us in an older covered motorboat. It wasn't as pretty, but it was definitely warmer. The ride over to the island was so much fun, our driver took a part of the roof off and invited me to stand up through the opening and take pictures of the lake and shore. Betty kept calling to me to be careful, but even she took a turn standing up and looking around. Our driver was so kind, he seemed really excited to be escorting five American women to the island. He seemed so pleased that I wanted to take his picture, he sat up straight and posed for me in such a cute way! On the way back, Mary Beth and I got a picture with him also.

Once on the island, we had to walk up to the church by way of a magnificent flight of steps. They were covered in moss and lichen and looked almost like part of the landscape. Mom and I were by this time old pros at going up and down large amounts of steps, but Betty needed some help to get all the way to the top. She was so proud that she was able to climb all 150 steps. I felt humbled to be in a place that my real great-grandmother had loved so much. It gave me a sense of belonging to something more than just America.

Imperial Palace

SUSPEND A KEEPSAKE

Instead of keeping foreign money or other small tokens in a pocket, hang it from your journaling box. Cut vertical strips from patterned paper (Club Scrap) for side borders on right and left pages. Add small strips on border edges cut from shimmer paper (Club Scrap). Mat photos on shimmer paper; adhere. Print title onto shimmer paper; mat with patterned paper and affix to center of both pages. Print journaling onto cardstock; mat with shimmer paper. Punch small holes in journaling box; string raffia through to hold coin from each end. Secure on back of journaling block; adhere to page.

Nancy Korf, Portland, Oregon

Trishaw Singapore

CREATE A CLAY ACCENT

Use air-dry clay for a wonderful theme-related accent on your pages. Mat patterned paper (Patchwork Paper Design) on red cardstock for background. Mat photo and adhere. Print title onto patterned paper; mat and adhere. For embellishment collages, start with pieces of mesh or screen. Add distressed gold and red papers and coins (Limited Edition Rubber Stamps). Use Chinese stamps (Plaid) on laminate chip; emboss with gold powder and adhere. Stamp into black air-dry clay (Ventura Craft); add holes for fiber. When dry, rub with metallic rub-ons; tie with fibers and mount on page.

Sara Horton, Brownwood, Texas

Egypt '84
WRAP WITH GAUZE

For a fun tribute to ancient Egyptian style, wrap page elements mummy-style. Tear corner piece from black cardstock; wrap in gauze and adhere to upper right corner. Ink slightly to age. Print large title letters; cut and mat. Add the year in hemp cord. Cut patterned paper in mountain pattern for bottom of page; tear matching cardstock and adhere. Tear photos and chalk edges; wrap in gauze, ink lightly and mount on bottom of page. Adhere remaining photos. Use letter stamps (Hero Arts) beneath photos to label.

Heidi Schueller, Waukesha, Wisconsin

Where Pharaohs Ruled The Land
FEATURE ANCIENT ARTWORK
IN A MODERN LAYOUT

Create a desert feel with distressed paper and netting. Mount distressed cardstock (Bazzill) onto background paper. Adhere coastal netting (Magic Scraps) to left side of page; stitch around four page edges. Scan painting, reduce to fit, and print in sepia onto vellum; sew onto page. String hemp twine with beads; attach with brads along left side. Print title onto patterned paper (Creative Imaginations); embellish with walnut ink (7 Gypsies) and sew onto page. Adhere the second word of title on distressed paper on title block with netting. Attach mini album made from patterned paper (Paper Adventures), cardstock and embellished with netting and beaded hemp trim.

Trudy Sigurdson, Victoria, British Columbia, Canada
Photos: Roy Wright, Victoria, British Columbia, Canada

The Holy Land
JOURNAL REFLECTIVE MOMENTS

Capture how a specific place on your vacation moved you. Mat trimmed, patterned paper (Creative Imaginations) with black cardstock. Enlarge, mat and adhere photo enlargement. Crop remaining photo; layer, mat with black cardstock and adhere. Label photos by printing place names on transparency film; emboss with gold powder and adhere over lower photos. For thistle crown, freehand draw and cut two thistled rings from wood-grained paper (source unknown); attach over journaling printed onto vellum and adhere with self-adhesive foam spacers. Print title; cut out, mat with black cardstock, and affix with adhesive foam spacers. Finish with glass bottle embellishment (7 Gypsies) filled with seed beads. Add cross sticker (EK Success) and adhere to page.

Denise Tucker, Versailles, Indiana
Photos: Ruth Walsh, Holton, Indiana

Israel
CREATE A SINGLE TITLE USING THREE SEPARATE TECHNIQUES

Journal about the special meaning of a particular place visited, such as the Wailing Wall. Print journaling; cut out and chalk edges. Wrap fiber and beads around lower edge, adhere on copper paper along with photo and mat with black velvet paper (Worldwin); mount on patterned paper (Hot Off The Press) background. Mat remaining photo with velvet paper; adhere. Affix freehand cut tags; set eyelets, tie with fibers and accent with beads. Create tiny Hebrew paper scrolls by photocopying or printing found text onto oatmeal paper. Roll small section of paper, tie with raffia and mount. Add curled and torn pieces of Hebrew text to tags, mounting one over strips of raffia. Computer-print large title letters onto copper cardstock; cut out with scissors or craft knife and mat with velvet paper. For second part of title, print onto cardstock; chalk and cut out each letter. Mount with brads and self-adhesive foam spacers. For last segment of title, print, tear edges and adhere.

Heidi Schueller, Waukesha, Wisconsin

The Temple Of The Gods

TELL A STORY

It is as important to document the story of a monument as it is to scrapbook the photo. Cut 1" strips from handmade paper (Bazzill) and adhere to background cardstock (Bazzill). Outline the outer edges of paper strips with silver pen. Enlarge photo and print with white border. Mat photo with blue paper; adhere. Affix silver beads above and below photo. Print title and journaling onto transparency film; trim and adhere on page.

Trudy Sigurdson, Victoria, British Columbia, Canada
Photo: Phyllis Wright, Victoria, British Columbia, Canada

Istanbul

USE FABRIC ON A PAGE

Lend the richness of fabric to your layouts. Sew distressed burgundy cardstock (Bazzill) onto black background. Layer fabric onto page, gathering sections to look like draped curtains, and sew along top of page with beaded trim. Separate fabric like curtains, wrap around lower page corners and adhere on back of page. Computer-print title onto cardstock. Cut out letters, emboss with gold powder and mat with black cardstock. Print journaling onto transparency film; emboss edges and mount on page with brads.

Trudy Sigurdson, Victoria, British Columbia, Canada
Photos: Roy Wright, Victoria, British Columbia, Canada

Africa

MAKE A COLLAGE FROM MEMORABILIA

Use a collage technique to incorporate souvenirs, documents, stamps and printed memorabilia from your trip into a single spread. Arrange items with title and banner stickers (NRN Designs) loosely for visual appeal, overlapping and allowing items to extend off cardstock edges. When content with the collage, permanently adhere all items in place. Once surfaces are covered, flip collages over and trim to desired size. Mount on background pages.

Nancy Korf, Portland, Oregon
Photos: Nancy Korf and Clint Olsen, Portland, Oregon

Africa

INCORPORATE PREPRINTED EMBELLISHMENTS

Using preprinted papers and embellishments is a great way to mimic the altered look on vacation layouts. Apply black photo corners to burlap paper (EK Success). Attach corner torn from faux stitched paper (EK Success) to upper corner of burlap paper. Add java weave (Jest Charming) to right side and coastal netting (Magic Scraps) to bottom left. Apply photo corners to one photo and tags with circle tags to another. Tear remaining photo; adhere all, using brads. where desired. Use vintage alphabet letter stickers (EK Success) and tags for title. Affix smaller tags on lower photo; write names and string with wire. Make envelope from handmade paper; embellish with coins and tags (EK Success). Insert memorabilia, journaling and remaining photos.

Polly McMillan, Bullhead City, Arizona

Western Australia

USE WRAPPING PAPER ON YOUR PAGES

Don't limit your gift wrap to packages, use it on a page. Tear corner section from stamp wrapping paper; adhere to background page. Use decorative scissors to cut out single stamp; adhere on page and add button embellishment. Mount photos. Print title and journaling onto patterned vellum (Worldwin); tear edges and adhere with brad fasteners. Mount photo on journaling block; top with slide mount. Finish with kangaroo-crossing sticker (EK Success).

Nancy McCoy, Gulfport, Mississippi

Natural Wonders

ADD NATURAL ELEMENTS TO YOUR LAYOUTS

For nature-inspired pages, use earthy elements for your embellishments. Adhere patterned paper (EK Success) to brown cardstock background (Bazzill). Double mat photos with cork (Magenta) and distressed cardstock. Leave length at end of cork to wrap around end of photo. Print identification and title onto transparency film. Cut out and affix to cork next to corresponding photos and at top for title. Poke holes for hemp; add stick and tie to page. For journaling, print onto transparency film; mount on cork and cardstock section; add matted photo. Set pair of eyelets into ends; mount on page and tie hemp through eyelets and around existing sticks. Complete page by adhering small sticks next to journaling and adding beaded hemp cord at top and bottom of page.

Trudy Sigurdson, Victoria, British Columbia, Canada
Photos: Colin Evans, Rayder, Wales, England

Córdoba, Argentina

USE A BROCHURE TO CREATE A FRAME

Use a brochure as a prominent page element instead of tucking it away in a pocket. Adhere main photo on light cardstock. Mount white paper over photo; tear out, snip and curl center to reveal photo. Cut out same opening from brochure with craft knife; mount over photo. Cut strip for title; add page pebble letters (Making Memories). Use the same technique for photo tag made from map paper. Use tickets to make tag for coins. Adhere memorabilia envelope (3L Corp.) to hold coins. Add date, page pebble and inked frame (K & Co.). Cut sections from ticket and map; adhere bottom of page. Mount journaling printed on transparency film over ticket and map sections with brad fasteners.

Kelli Noto, Centennial, Colorado

Paraguay

DESIGN A MOSAIC BORDER WITH STICKERS

Using these tile stickers is a great way to make a mosaic border without the weight of real tiles. Mount fabric border across top of background page with self-adhesive foam spacers. Mat photos with textured papers (Sizzix); adhere. Cut square tile stickers (EK Success) in half diagonally to create small triangles; affix on lower page in mosaic pattern. Computer-print title on cardstock; cut out and adhere. Print journaling onto textured paper; distress and mount.

Shannon Taylor, Bristol, Tennessee

Tulum
STAMP AN INTERESTING BORDER

A unique border is easily created with these Mayan stamps (Chronicle Books). Print journaling onto green cardstock and adhere to tan cardstock; tear and mount on left page. Print out title on cardstock; cut out and adhere on first page. Stamp border around edges of tan cardstock; tear into strips leaving one in "L" shape. Chalk and mount as borders on all three pages. Crop and mat photos as desired; adhere. Punch desired photos with jumbo square punch; mount onto background pages over torn paper strip. Add studs (Scrapworks). For journaling, create pocket that will hold several photos; embellish on outside with stamped paper strip. Print journaling blocks onto vellum and trim to photo and additional photos; mount over photos and tie photos together with fiber. Adhere small Velcro piece to back of cards and other side of page to keep cards from falling out.

Beth Rogers, Mesa, Arizona

Cathedral Metropolitana

DISTRESS A PHOTO

Sand the edges of your photo to give it an aged and distressed look. Begin by trimming and distressing patterned paper (Daisy D's); mount on cardstock background (Bazzill). Apply strips of mesh (Magic Mesh) all over page. Attach binding tape strip with large brad fasteners to left side. Enlarge photo; use fine sand-paper to distress edges and affix over mesh and cotton binding (source unknown). Computer print title and caption onto brown cardstock; cut out and ink edges. Set eyelet in title bar, tie with jute and adhere to bottom of page with large snap. Affix letters off-set onto torn distressed paper. Add bead rocks (source unknown) with glue as desired. Finish by mounting silver medallion (Accent It!) on mesh (Magenta).

Trudy Sigurdson, Victoria, British Columbia, Canada
Photos: Laureen Brain, Victoria, British Columbia, Canada

Mexico

HOUSE ADDITIONAL PHOTOS IN A POCKET

A great way to include many pictures in one page is to house them inside a photo pocket. Adhere panoramic photo to green cardstock. Tear a section of metallic gold cardstock vertically. Using jumbo sun punch (Emagination Crafts), punch only partially through top of torn gold cardstock, pulling sun "rays" out for dimension. Print journaling onto vellum and tear vertically; mount on gold cardstock with brad fasteners. Punch sun shape through both vellum and gold cardstock. Adhere border journaling strip to page. String metal beads (Westrim Crafts) onto wire; mount under photo by inserting wire through page beneath journaling section and secur-ing other end behind page. Cut section from metallic gold cardstock for photo pocket; distress by crumpling. Open and tear and roll top edge of pocket. Cut slits into lower right corner; bend back and distress edges. Heat emboss title with gold powder onto small piece of green cardstock; affix behind opening of pocket. Attach bottom edge and sides of pocket with brad fasteners. Tie photos together with fibers and slip into pocket.

Emily Curry Hitchingham, Memory Makers Books

Belleza Latina

MANIPULATE TEXT

Use a program such as Print Explosion to place text onto an enlarged photo. Enlarge photo; place title at top of photo and journaling on left side vertically. Print and cut out. Adhere to background cardstock (Bazzill). Cut strips from lighter-colored cardstocks; mount to page, crossing at lower right corner. Triple mat photo; adhere. To re-create the look of the title and journaling in a traditional scrapbook style, simply print title and journaling on transparency film, emboss with white ink and mount over enlarged and cropped photo.

Wanda E. Santiago–Cintron, Deerfield, Wisconsin

Belleza Boricua

CREATE A DIGITAL LAYOUT

This botanical-inspired digital layout was created in Corel Draw. Start with foreground photo. Remove sections exposing background images. Add text. To re-create this layout as a traditional scrapbook page, use an enlarged foreground photo as frame for standard-sized background photo. Cut away area to expose photo. For added feathering effect, adhere torn mulberry atop photo so edges can be seen through frame. Ideas for title and journaling are: stamping onto frame, printing onto vellum, printing and embossing onto vellum, and printing onto transparency film.

Wanda E. Santigo–Cintron, Deerfield, Wisconsin

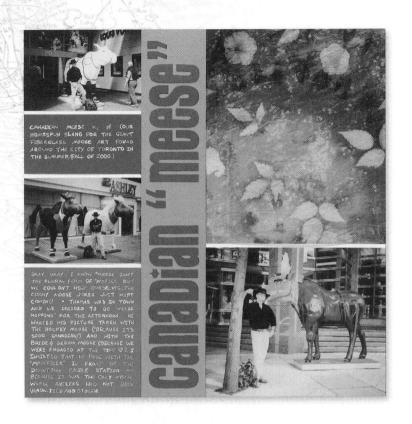

Canadian "Meese"

USE A BLOCKING TECHNIQUE

Re-size photos to fit the blocking style you like. Print journaling onto cardstock in light gray; trace over with white pen. Cut patterned paper (Paper Adventures), photos and journaling blocks to size. Adhere all on white cardstock, leaving some cardstock peeking through for added effect. Use craft knife to cut computer-printed title from cardstock; mount on yellow cardstock (Bazzill) and adhere title strip to page.

Leah Blanco Williams, Kansas City, Missouri

The Garden City

FEATURE DRIED FLOWERS

Embellish a title with dried flowers for a pretty look. Cut section from pale yellow paper; adhere to right side of green cardstock background (Bazzill) and cover in mesh (Magenta). Tear large section from green patterned paper (K & Co.); stitch onto page. Mat photos; adhere horizontal photos on page and mount vertical photo with self-adhesive foam spacers. Print journaling onto vellum; adhere to page. For title, affix mesh to page. Use craft knife to cut computer-printed title; adhere to mesh with dried flowers and dragonfly button (source unknown). Finish by stamping date (Making Memories) below vertical photo and adding nailheads (Chatterbox) around page edges.

Trudy Sigurdson, Victoria, British Columbia, Canada

Additional Instructions & Credits

COVER PARIS

Mat blue textured cardstock (Club Scrap) to brown textured cardstock (Club Scrap) to form background. Tear sections from patterned paper (PSX Design); adhere to page. Triple mat photo and mount with various embellishments, such as distressed and altered papers, clock hands, luggage strap, and watch crystals (Germanow-Simon Mach Co.). Stamp domino tiles (Club Scrap) with StazOn ink (Tsukineko); adhere to page. Finish with 3-D stickers (EK Success).

Jodi Amidei, Memory Makers
Photo: Kelli Noto, Centennial, Colorado

PAGE 3 BOOKPLATE

Freehand-draw suitcase and cut from light brown handmade paper (Heartstrings). Cut top and side portions of suitcase from darker brown handmade paper; adhere to suitcase pattern. Create straps with buckles (Making Memories) and corner embellishments from suede paper (Paper Adventures); detail with "stitching" using black pen. Create handle by cutting small circle frame (K & Co.) in half using wire cutters. Adorn suitcase with travel stickers (Mrs. Grossman's) that have been scanned, shrunk and aged with sepia ink.

PAGE 6 BON VOYAGE

Stamp (Crafts Etc, Stampendous!) patterned cardstock (Club Scrap) with watermark Ink (Tsukineko); emboss with silver embossing powder. Mat patterned cardstock on gray and brown cardstocks. Create photo frames from brown cardstock; coat with several layers of clear extra thick embossing powder. After cooling, repeat stamping technique by heat embossing with silver powder until just melted; allow to cool, then bend to crackle. Tear interior edges of larger focal frame; coat frame with several layers of extra thick embossing powder, with the exception of torn edges. Repeat embossing and crackling technique as before. Embellish frame corners with brads, adhere to photos with self-adhesive foam spacers and mount to page. Computer journal passage and names on brown cardstock; affix to page with brads and metal nameplates (Magic Scraps) for individual pictures. Create title with computer fonts on brown cardstock; repeat embossing and crackling technique. Embellish left page border with strip of wire screen, brads, fibers and woven lables (Me & My Big Ideas) in name plates.

PAGE 14 AIT

Trim pieces of map paper; mount to page. To make distressed paper, spray brown cardstock; crumple. Open and chalk creases to age. Heat emboss edges in gold. Use freehand journaling for effect. Cut altered photo; mat under gold embossed metal frame and on top of gold mesh. String chalked letter tags; attach with gold brads. Emboss photo corner; attach along with beads and shell to matted photo. Adhere mesh to upper left corner of page; add charm. Embellish lower left corner with distressed paper, gold mesh and embossed frames hanging from matted picture by gold brad. Add embellishments as desired. Make faux shaker box from gold embossed frame. Start with blue background, add torn brown cardstock, beads and popped shell cut-outs.

Heather Border, Kuna, Idaho

PAGE 38 FROM THE MASTER'S HAND...PARADISE

Mat purple paper to blue cardstock background (DMD) with pewter eyelets. Double mat enlarged photo; adhere with eyelets. Affix to page smaller matted photo and double-matted journaling printed onto transparency; add metal photo corners (Making Memories). Set eyelets outside top corners of main photo; string leather lacing through all eyelets. Print title onto cardstock; tear out, chalk and adhere with metal washer words (Making Memories), brads and feather charms (Halcraft). Finish with more washer words, tied and matted metal tag (K & Co.), and photo corners with glued feather charms on top for background page corner embellishment.

Andrea Lyn Vetten-Marley, Aurora, Colorado
Photos: Jodi and Tom Amidei, Lafayette, Colorado

PAGE 60 SEA WORLD

Print title and journaling onto vellum. Cut out title block leaving length below for cropped photos. Cut out circle section from desired photo; adhere to top left corner of paper (Karen Foster Design). Mount vellum title atop photo; secure by stitching with buttons. Add cropped photos to vellum below title; mount remaining photos and journaling.

Diana Hudson, Bakersfield, California

PAGE 82 LAND OF THE FREE

Cut horizontal sections from red patterned paper (C-Thru Ruler); adhere to tan background page. Make page corners from blue patterned paper (Karen Foster Design); adhere with buttons (Hillcreek Designs). Double mat main photo; tear bottom edge from top mat; mount with foam tape. Mount remaining matted photo. Cut stars from blue patterned paper; affix to page. Age circle tags with walnut ink, stamp (Hero Arts) and affix over stars created using template (Deluxe Designs) with buttons. Print journaling onto transparencies; cut out and paint backsides with acrylic paint; mat to blue patterned paper; adhere to page.

Brandi Ginn, Lafayette, Colorado
Photos: Amy Brasier, Erie, Colorado

PAGE 104 TAJ MAHAL

Mat a light green cardstock to dark green for background. Tear a horizontal section from dark green cardstock; adhere to page. Freehand draw monument; use chalks and pens to accent; cut out and adhere with foam tape. Mat and mount photo; add photo corners (Global Solutions). Print title onto vellum; tear out and adhere to monument. Print journaling in scroll shape; cut out, chalk, and mount with peacock feathers to page.

Janice Scott, Evergreen, Colorado
Photos: Peggy Scott, Evergreen, Colorado

CONTRIBUTING MEMORY MAKERS MASTERS

Valerie Barton, Joanna Bolick, Lisa Dixon, Brandi Ginn, Dianna Graham, Diana Hudson, Torrey Miller, Kelli Noto, Michelle Pesce, Heidi Schueller, Trudy Sigurdson, Denise Tucker, Andrea Lyn Vetten-Marley, Holle Wiktorek

Sources

The following companies manufacture products showcased on scrapbook pages featured within this book. Please check your local retailers to find these materials. We have made every attempt to properly credit the items mentioned in this book and apologize to those we may have missed.

2DYE4
(519) 537-6756
www.canscrapink.com

3L Corp.
(800) 828-3130
www.3lcorp.com

7 Gypsies
(480) 325-3358
www.7gypsies.com

A Charming Place
www.acharmingplace.com

Accent It!- no contact info available

Accu-Cut® (wholesale only)
(800) 288-1670
www.accucut.com

Adobe
www.adobe.com

All My Memories
(888) 553-1998
www.allmymemories.com

All Night Media (see Plaid Enterprises)

All The Extras
www.alltheextras.com

American Art Clay Co. (AMACO)
(800) 374-1600
www.amaco.com

Amscan, Inc.
(800) 444-8887
www.amscan.com

Anima Designs
(800) 570-6847
www.animadesigns.com

Artistic Scrapper
(818) 786-8304
www.artisticscrapper.com

Autumn Leaves
(800) 588-6707
www.autumnleaves.com

Avery
(800) GO-AVERY
www.avery.com

Back Street, Inc
(678) 206-7373
www.backstreetcrafts.com

Bag of Beach- no contact info available

Bazzill Basics Paper
(480) 58-8557
www.bazzilbasics.com

Boutique Trims (wholesale only)
(248) 437-2017
www.boutiquetrims.com

Canson Inc..®
(800) 628-9283
www.canson-us.com

CARL Mfg. USA, Inc.
(wholesale only)
(800) 257-4771
www.Carl-Products.com

Chatterbox, Inc.
(208) 939-9133
www.chatterboxinc.com

Chronicle Books
www.chroniclebooks.com

Chronicle Stamps-no contact info available

Clearsnap®, Inc.
(wholesale only)
(800) 448-4862
www.clearsnap.com

Cloud 9 Design™
(763) 493-0990
www.cloud9design.biz

Club Scrap™, Inc.
(888) 634-9100
www.clubscrap.com

Cock-A-Doodle Design, Inc.
(800) 262-9727
www.cockadoodledesign.com

Colorbök™, Inc.
(wholesale only)
(800) 366-4660
www.colorbok.com

Colors By Design
(800) 832-8436
www.colorsbydesign.com

Crafts Etc.
www.craftsetc.com

Craf-T Products
(507) 235-3996
www.craf-tproducts.com

Creative Imaginations
(wholesale only)
(800) 942-6487
www.cigift.com

Creative Impressions
(719) 596-4860
www.creativeimpressions.com

Creative Memories®
(800) 468-9335
www.creativememories.com

C-Thru® Ruler Company, The
(wholesale only)
(800) 243-8419
www.cthruruler.com

Czech Beads (wholesale only)
www.czechbeads.com

Daisy D's Paper Company
(888) 601-8955
www.daisydspaper.com

Darice, Inc.
(800) 321-1494
www.darice.com

Delta Technical Coatings, Inc.
(800) 423-4135
www.deltacrafts.com

Deluxe Designs
(480) 497-9005
www.deluxecuts.com

Design Originals
(800) 877-7820
www.d-originals.com

Design Templates Library
- no contact info available

Die Cuts With A View
(801) 224-6766
www.diecutswithaview.com

DJ Inkers
(800) 325-4890
www.djinkers.com

DMC Corp.
(973) 589-0606
www.dmc-usa.com

DMD Industries, Inc.
(wholesale only)
(800) 805-9890
www.dmdind.com

Dolphin Enterprises
(801) 495-7234
www.protect-a-page.com

Doodlebug Design Inc.™
(801) 966-9952

Duncan Enterprises
(559) 294-3282
www.duncan-enterprises.com

Dymo
www.dymo.com

EK Success™, Ltd.
(800) 524-1349
www.eksuccess.com

Emagination Crafts, Inc.
(wholesale only)
(630) 833-9521
www.emaginationcrafts.com

Family Treasures Inc. ®
www.familytreasures.com

Far and Away
(549) 340-0124
www.farandawayscrapbooks.com

Fibers by the Yard
(800) 760-8901
www.fibersbytheyard.com

Fiskars, Inc. (wholesale only)
(715) 842-2091
www.fiskars.com

FoofaLa
(402) 330-3208
www.foofala.com

Frances Meyer, Inc.
(800) 372-6237
www.francesmeyer.com

Germanow-Simon Mach Co.-
no contact info available

Global Solutions
(206) 343-5210
www.globalsolutionsonline.com

Grafix® Graphic Art Systems, Inc.
(800) 447-2349
www.grafixarts.com

Halcraft USA, Inc.
(212) 367-1580
www.halcraft.com

Heartstrings-no contact info available

Hero Arts® Rubber Stamps, Inc.
(wholesale only)
(800) 822-4376
www.heroarts.com

Hot Off The Press, Inc.
(800) 227-9595
www.paperpizzaz.com

Ilford Imaging USA, Inc.
(888) 727-4751
www.printasiafun.com

Impress Rubber Stamps
(206) 901-9101
www.impressrubberstamps.com

Inkadinkado® Rubber Stamps
(800) 888-4652
www.inkadinkado.com

Jacquard Products
(707) 433-9577
www.jacquardproducts.com

Jean Allen- no contact info available

Jesse James and Co.
(610) 435-0201
www.jessejamesbutton.com

Jest Charming
www.jestcharming.com

JewelCraft, LLC
(201) 223-0804
www.jewelcraft.biz

JHB International
(800) 525-9007
www.buttons.com

JudiKins
(310) 515-1115
www.judikins.com

K & B Innovations
www.shrinkydinks.com

K & Company
(888) 244-2083
www.kandcompany.com

Karen Foster Design™
(wholesale only)
(801) 451-9779
www.karenfosterdesign.com

Keeping Memories Alive™
(800) 419-4949
www.scrapbooks.com

KI Memories
www.kimemories.com

Krylon
(216) 515-7693
www.krylon.com

Lettering Delights
www.letteringdelights.com

Lil Davis Designs
(949) 838-0344
www.lildavisdesigns.com

Limited Edition Rubberstamps
(650) 594-4242
www.limitededitionrs.com

Lineco
(800) 336-4847
www.lineco.com

Magenta Rubber Stamps
(wholesale only)
(800) 565-5254
www.magentarubberstamps.com

Magic Mesh™
(651) 345-6374
www.magicmesh.com

Magic Scraps™
(972) 238-1838
www.magicsraps.com

Making Memories
(800) 286-5263
www.makingmemories.com

Marvy® Uchida (wholesale only)
(800) 541-5877
www.uchida.com

McGill Inc.
(800) 982-9884
www.mcgillinc.com

Me & My Big Ideas
(wholesale only)
(949) 589-4607
www.meandmybigideas.com

Merriam-Webster
www.merriamwebster.com

Metropolis Paper Company
- no contact info available

Michelin English Edition Maps
- no contact info available

Mrs. Grossman's Paper Co.
(wholesale only)
(800) 429-4549
www.mrsgrossmans.com

Northern Spy
(530) 620-7430
www.northernspy.com

NRN Designs
(800) 421-6988
www.nrndesigns.com

Nunn Design
(360) 379-3557
www.nunndesign.com

Paper Adventures®
(wholesale only)
(800) 727-0699
www.paperadventures.com

Paper Garden, The
(wholesale only)
(702) 639-1956
www.mypapergarden.com

Paper Loft, The (wholesale only)
(866) 254-1961
www.paperloft.com

Papyrus- no contact info available

Patchwork Paper Design
(480) 515-0537
www.patchworkpaper.com

Pebbles, Inc.
www.pebblesinc.com

Penny Black Rubber Stamps
(510) 849-1883

Pioneer Photo Albums, Inc.®
(800) 366-3686
www.pioneerphotoalbums.com

Plaid Enterprises, Inc
(800) 842-4197
www.plaidonline.com

Polyform Products
(847) 427-0020
www.polyformproducts.com

Post Modern Design- no contact info available

Printasia (see Ilford Imaging)

Prismacolor-no contact info available

Provo Craft® (wholesale only)
(888) 577-3545
www.provocraft.com

PSX Design™
(800) 782-6748
www.psxdesign.com

Punch Bunch, The
(254) 791-4209
www.thepunchbunch.com

Pulsar Eco-Products LLC
(888) 295-9297
www.pulsarpaper.com

Quick Point- no contact info available

QuicKutz®
(888) 702-1146
www.quickutz.com

Ranger Industries, Inc.
(800) 244-2211
www.rangerink.com

Rollbind®, Inc.
(800) 438-3542
www.rollabind.com

Rubber Stampede
(800) 423-4135
www.rubberstampede.com

Rusty Pickle
(801) 274-9588
www.rustypickle.com

Sakura of America
(800) 776-6257
www.gellyroll.com

Sandylion Sticker Designs (wholesale only)
(800) 387-4215
www.sandylion.com

Sarah Heidt Photo Craft LLC
(734) 424-2776
www.SarahHeidtPhotoCraft.com

Schlage- no contact info available

Scrap Arts (wholesale only)
(503) 631-4893
www.scraparts.com

Scrap Ease® (What's New LTD)
(wholesale only)
(800) 272-3874
www.whatsnewltd.com

Scrapbook Diva
(619) 235-6789
www.scrapbookdiva.com

Scrap Pagerz™
(435) 645-0696
www.scrappagerz.com

Scrapworks, LLC
(713) 842-2547
www.scrapworksllc.com

Scrapyard 329
(775) 829-1118
www.scrapyard329.com

SEI, Inc.
(800) 333-3279
www.shopsei.com

Sizzix
(866) 742-4447
www.sizzix.com

Stamp Doctor, The
(208) 342-4362
www.stampdoctor.com

Stampabilities
(405) 745-1218
www.stampabilities.com

Stampendous!®
(800) 869-0474
www.stampendous.com

Stampers Anonymous/The Creative Block
(440) 333-7942

Stampin' Up!®
(800) 782-6787
www.stampinup.com

Staples
www.staples.com

Suze Weinberg Design Studio
(732) 761-2400
www.schmoozewithsuze.com

Sweetwater
(970) 867-4428
www.sweetwaterscrapbook.com

Tandy Leather Company
(800) 433-3201
www.tandyleather.com

Tsukineko®, Inc.
(800) 769-6633
www.tsukineko.com

USArtQuest
(800) 200-7848
www.usartquest.com

U.S. Shell Inc.
(856) 943-1709
www.usshell.com

Ventura Craft- no contact info available

Westrim Crafts
(800) 727-2727
www.westrim.com

Woodland Scenics
(573) 346-5555
www.woodlandscenics.com

Wordsworth
(719) 282-3495
www.wordsworthstamps.com

Worldwin Papers (CTI)
(888) 843-6455
www.thepapermill.com

Wubie Prints
(888) 256-0107
www.wubieprints.com

Yvonne Albritton Designs
www.yvonnealbritton.com

Web Sites

Fodors Focus on Photography
www.fodors.com/focus/

Two Peas In A Bucket
www.twopeasinabucket.com

Index